# THE COMPLETE GUIDE TO
# BARRIER-FREE HOUSING

## Convenient Living for the Elderly and the Physically Handicapped

### GARY D. BRANSON

Hilary W. Swinson
**Contributing Editor**

BETTERWAY PUBLICATIONS, INC.
WHITE HALL, VIRGINIA

Published by Betterway Publications, Inc.
P.O. Box 219
Crozet, VA 22932
(804) 823-5661

Cover photograph courtesy of Homestyles Plan Service
Typography by Park Lane Associates

Branson, Gary D.
   The complete guide to barrier-free housing : convenient living for the elderly and physically handicapped / Gary D. Branson ; Hilary W. Swinson, contributing editor
       p.  cm.
   Includes index.
   ISBN 1-55870-188-5 (paperback) : $14.95
   1. Architecture and the aged.  2. Architecture and the handicapped.  I. Title.
   NA2545.A3B7  1991
   720'.42--dc20                                        90-21761
                                                        CIP

Printed in the United States of America
0 9 8 7 6 5 4 3 2

*Dedicated to*

*Gale Olson*

*A Friend for first thoughts*

# Acknowledgments

Our thanks to Bob Hostage, Hilary Swinson, Jackie Hostage, Tim Sams, and all the folks at Betterway.

## ABOUT THE HOUSE ON THE COVER

This design, the first "Adaptable House," has gained national recognition. Endorsed by the National Association of Home Builders, a model home built from the design was one of nine award-winning homes featured in the 1988 Street of Dreams home tour.

Aptly termed the "Adaptable Home," the design can be changed as the physical needs of people change, whether due to accident, illness, or age. It is spacious, modern, and elegant.

Living Design, the architectural firm that developed this plan, took special care to ensure that the home is wheelchair-accessible. The front walk slopes gently to the double-door entry. The spacious foyer allows plenty of turning area to accommodate wheelchairs. All hallways are 48 inches wide, and doors are 36 inches wide with easy to grasp, lever-type door handles.

Throughout the home, there are features that will be appreciated by everyone, including light switches no higher than 4 feet from the floor, low, easy to open casement windows, and adjustable shelves and clothing rods in all of the closets. The garage doors, equipped with automatic door openers, are 8 feet high to accommodate vans. A ramp leads from the garage to the utility room.

The kitchen is designed with pull-out shelving, lower cabinets and counter work areas, a large pantry closet, and an island cooktop. The outdoors can be enjoyed on the large backyard deck, with access from the nook and the master bedroom. A raised-bed planting area off the deck makes gardening a pleasure that can be enjoyed by all.

The master bedroom features a spa tub, an oversized, wheelchair-accessible shower, and dual vanities. Another full bath is adjacent to the remaining two bedrooms, and a powder room is off the hall leading to the major living areas.

The family room, dining room, and living room are separated by wall sections adorned with stately columns. Two fireplaces and luxurious window treatments bring in light and warmth. The den also features a bay window. The ceilings in all of these rooms are over 11 feet high.

This design has 2,844 square feet of livable, adaptable space. For an informational brochure or to order plan books and blueprints, call (800) 547-5570, in Minnesota (612) 927-6707, or write Homestyles Plan Service, 6800 France Avenue South, Suite 115, Minneapolis, MN 55435.

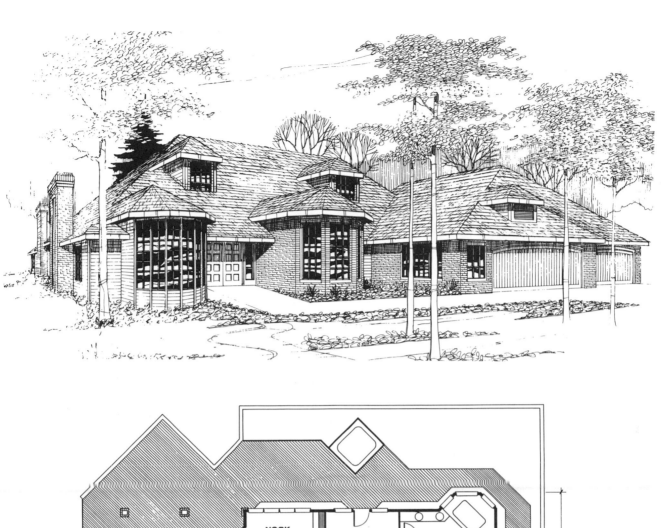

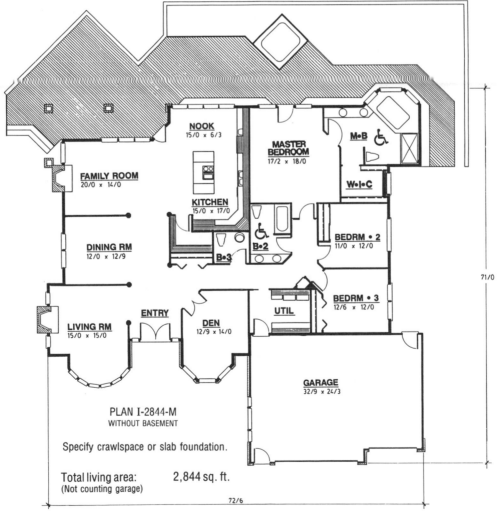

**FAMILY ROOM**
20/0 x 14/0

**NOOK**
15/0 x 6/3

**MASTER BEDROOM**
17/2 x 18/0

**M•B**

**KITCHEN**
15/0 x 17/0

**W•I•C**

**DINING RM**
12/0 x 12/9

**B•2**

**B•3**

**BEDRM • 2**
11/0 x 12/0

**LIVING RM**
15/0 x 15/0

**ENTRY**

**DEN**
12/9 x 14/0

**UTIL**

**BEDRM • 3**
12/6 x 12/0

71/0

**GARAGE**
32/9 x 24/3

PLAN I-2844-M
WITHOUT BASEMENT

Specify crawlspace or slab foundation.

Total living area:     2,844 sq. ft.
(Not counting garage)

72/6

# Contents

# Introduction

My father put me to work on a construction gang as soon as I was big enough to carry a 5-gallon pail of paint. He taught me much of what I know about building, and for more than forty years I have made my livelihood from the housing industry.

In addition to construction, my father also taught me the difference between friends and acquaintances. A friend is someone who will loan you money without asking why you need it, someone who knows everything about you and likes you anyway. You will have many acquaintances, but you will meet few people who will go to the well with you.

To just such a friend I have dedicated this book. Gale Olson was a South Dakota farm boy who joined an airborne unit at Fort Bragg when he graduated high school at age eighteen. He raced motorcycles and won trophies doing it. Then, as a young family man, Gale was struck by lupus arthritis and spent the last years of his life in a wheelchair.

I helped Gale remodel his two-story farm house, building a bedroom and bath on the first floor so it was accessible. Refusing to yield to his problem, Gale wore out several wheelchairs. I helped him stay mobile by aiding him in shopping trips, and I learned firsthand of the barriers that face those who have physical limitations. (Gale would have rejected any charge of "handicaps": he had more guts than a blind bull-fighter, and fought to stay active. His doctor gave him five years to live when he was diagnosed. Gale lived another thirteen years.)

This summer my mother passed away, the victim of advanced years and Parkinson's disease. At her funeral I renewed acquaintanceship with aunts and uncles who are living with arthritis, strokes, and allied maladies. We are a graying family — and nation.

Several years ago during an editorial meeting, I proposed that the magazine for which I wrote do a series of articles on making houses more easily accessible. A colleague hooted: "How many handicapped people do you think there are?" At the time I could not reply. Today, I have that answer: 43 million. Depending on how you define the term "handicapped," there are an estimated 43 million people in the U.S. who have some limits to their mobility. In my home state of Minnesota an estimated one out of four families has a family member who has some physical limitations.

We are also an aging nation. Recent estimates show that, within the next decade or two, half our citizens will be age sixty — or older. We have all become more acutely aware of how inaccessible our buildings are, because we all are aging.

Nor is that the entire picture. As one young person — a paraplegic man who was demonstrating kitchen cabinet accessibility at the builder's show — pointed out, the college student who breaks a leg while skiing on winter break will learn that the world was built for the able-bodied. This is ridiculous: Tens of thousands of us are injured each year in bathroom accidents. Slippery floors and bathtubs are dangerous to all; stair rails that come loose under the weight of a falling person are built so that they fail their only purpose: preventing accidents and injuries.

We are not talking here of radical or unusual housing designs. We are suggesting that all housing should be built with an emphasis on maximum convenience, safety, and accessibility for everyone.

Recent polls show that people today (86 percent) prefer to "age in place," or to continue to live as independently as possible in their own homes. Advancing age does not end or alter the desire for home ownership: privacy, freedom, comfort, and a bit of dirt to dig in are universal longings.

Polls also show that people are willing to pay extra for those items that will help make homes more accessible. Who has not wished for a shelf by an entry door, on which to rest packages while unlocking the door? Who would not welcome the addition of a porch with a roof to shelter us from the elements while we enter? Who has not been frustrated by the hard-to-find light switch, the slippery bathroom floor, the steep or narrow stairs that invite an accident? And should we be satisfied to reflect that the most dangerous place to be is in our own homes?

Today, an entire industry is discovering that too little thought has been given in the past to making houses accessible to all. It is not enough to make a particular house fit the needs of its particular handicapped or less able occupant. The barriers we build into houses are a menace to us all, and cost us untold millions of dollars in insurance payments for home injuries.

To remove the barriers in housing, we need to address several problems. First, it is just good sense to make homes as convenient and accessible as possible. This means removing all barriers. Next, we should build with materials that reduce or eliminate home maintenance expenses. There is little we can do about the cost of building a house, but there is much we can do to reduce the cost of *living* in that house. We can choose building materials more carefully, to avoid frequent repainting, to avoid frequent replacement of roofing, and to avoid frequent repair bills for appliances. We need to work toward quality in building materials, following the recognition that quality does not cost, it pays.

There is one other housing expense, one that we can do much to control. That is the monthly utility cost of operating a house. Energy costs already have soared, then settled back. But recent developments indicate that we are about to take another roller-coaster ride on energy costs.

Unhappily, many or most senior citizens live in houses bought several decades ago. They live with outdated heating equipment, equipment that is very inefficient. Most houses that are twenty or more years old have inadequate insulation, weathered and leaking windows, and cracked caulk that lets the weather in.

Our appliances were built before there was an industry regard for efficiency. If your appliances do not show an energy efficiency rating (EER) label, you are probably wasting a good deal of money on energy. Updating a furnace, water heater, and refrigerator could return a big savings on monthly utility bills that are real budget-wreckers for those on a fixed income.

Polls show that those on fixed incomes have a real struggle with unforeseen charges for home maintenance. Utility bills that were once nuisance bills, hardly worthy of consideration, now take major bites out of our incomes. While we are removing the barriers from housing, we should not neglect the problems of affordability of maintenance and utilities.

## WHO ARE THE DISABLED?

The term "disabled" may often be mistaken to mean those with easily perceived handicaps: those who require walkers or wheelchairs to get around, who carry a white cane or lead a guide dog, or who need an assistant to move about. But the disabled also include any persons who are unable to perform routine physical acts without difficulty. These routine acts include seeing, walking, hearing, breathing, doing everyday manual chores, and caring for oneself. The U.S. Census Bureau in a study that was conducted in 1984-85 concluded that more than 37 million people had one or more of the above limitations, in the over fifteen year age group, while an estimated five million disabled persons are children. If we include the additional one million institutionalized people, we have a total of 43 million people with some form of physical disability.

That, however, is not the entire picture. Our aging population is growing, so that impairments associated with age may be gaining in numbers at a geometric rate. Diseases such as cancer and Parkinson's disease claim a growing number of victims, with few cures in sight.

President Bush has signed the "Americans with Disabilities Act" to prohibit discrimination against the disabled. Government from local to national levels is passing and/or considering bills that would help the less able pay for needed remodeling or maintenance for their homes. We should all voice support for these policies. In the words of John Donne: "Send not to know for whom the bell tolls; It tolls for thee."

# 1
# The Home's Exterior

When building or remodeling to remove access barriers, you must obviously begin with the exterior of the house.

## SELECTING THE LOT

The selection of the lot is all-important. A steep lot with many steps at the porch and walks is obviously poorly suited to good access. Keep in mind also that a sloped lawn will be harder to maintain. If you must build on such a lot, your only option might be regrading to create a system of retaining walls and terraces, as well as ramps for access to the house itself. A lot that slopes toward the street can also be graded to permit a front walkout through the basement level. Inside, you can build wide stairways, perhaps fitted with chairlifts or even an elevator, to move persons in wheelchairs to a second level, one that might open at ground level on an uphill terrace.

## DRIVES

If kept in good repair either blacktop (asphalt) or concrete can be a suitable driveway material. Making the drive area more accessible requires that the drive be built wider than is usual, so car doors or the side doors on passenger vans can be fully opened for adequate access. For double driveways a width of 24 feet will permit parking two cars side by side, plus providing enough room so a person can exit the car or van on the drive, and enter a waiting wheelchair, without stepping onto the lawn on one side or banging car doors on the other.

Blacktop (asphalt) surfaces provide good slip-free footing if kept clear of snow and ice. A drive that slopes gently toward the afternoon sun (to the south) will catch more solar gain and will keep ice and snow melted in winter.

Concrete drives can be finished with a rough texture, rather than having a smooth trowel finish, for better traction underfoot. After the concrete is troweled it can be gone over with a rough-bristle broom such as those used for maintenance or for barns. Brooming a concrete surface is done when the concrete has hardened slightly but is still soft enough to apply the texture.

### Driveway Finish

Another option for finishing drives to be slip-proof is to use an exposed aggregate finish. An exposed aggregate slab can be made by any of several methods: you can form and pour the slab, then scatter aggregate such as gravel, quartz, or granite on the surface. The aggregate is then tamped down into the fresh concrete. When the concrete has firmed, the surface is pressure-washed to remove the concrete and to expose the aggregate. Optionally, the aggregate can be added to the concrete mix at the plant, and the surface concrete washed away after the slab has been leveled and is firm.

For best access, driveway finishes such as cobblestone and any deep joints or pattern should be avoided. Surfaces that are very uneven present a walking hazard to those who are unsure or unsteady on their feet, and may present difficulty for anyone who uses a walking aid or a wheelchair.

All driveway surfaces should be kept free of dirt, oil, and stray objects that might impede free travel.

## GARAGE

A double overhead garage door provides the easiest access, rather than using a series of single garage doors. Door height should be sufficient to allow a passenger van to enter. My own minivan, a Ford Aerostar, requires a garage door height of 6½ feet (78 inches) for entry, but full-size vans used for medical ambulances may require full 8-foot high garage doors.

Garage door openers are almost a standard equipment item in modern houses and are even more desirable for those with limited access. The garage door opener provides convenience, safety, and lighting at the push of a button. The opener does all the work of lifting the door, eliminates the driver having to get out of the car and into the weather to open the door, and lets the driver and passengers gain the safety of a closed, lighted garage before exiting the vehicle. In addition, it is difficult for an intruder to open a garage door that has an automatic opener. Other options on the door controls include the ability to turn on lights inside the house before you enter.

The width of the garage should be such that you

can park two vehicles side by side and still have a minimum of 3 feet between vehicles — more is better, if you plan for wheelchair access. Vans will be almost 6 feet wide, and if you allow for 3 feet on each side, plus 3 feet between the vehicles, you arrive at a combined 21 feet. For a garage that will be used by a wheelchair occupant, it is best to provide 24 feet of width in the garage.

Garage floors and drives should be kept sealed, whether they are concrete or blacktop. A sealed surface will let occupants wipe away any oil or grease drips, to keep the slab dry and free from falling hazards.

## WALKS

Most entry walks that connect the street and house are 4 or 5 feet wide, and will easily accommodate a wheelchair. Service walks to the sides or rear of the house, however, are usually only 2 or 3 feet wide. A 3-foot wide walk will permit passage by a wheelchair, but walks that are narrower should be broken out and relaid. Also, any walk that is cracked or heaved from frost or erosion should be broken out and relaid to avoid any stumbling blocks.

Like driveways, walks can be concrete, either aggregate or broom-finished. Again, walks of loose-laid paving bricks (laid on a sand base with sand swept into the joints) may prove to be a walking hazard to the infirm, because such bricks can tilt and become uneven when weathered.

## STEPS AND RAMPS

Steps should be built at least as wide as the walk and entry they serve, usually at least 4 feet wide. But steps can be replaced by a ramp or a step ramp to make passage easier. A ramp is usually of concrete but can be built of wood. For a steep slope you can interrupt a flight of stairs or a long

*A garage door opener provides convenience, ease of entry, comfort, and safety at little cost. Look for an automatic opener that lights the garage interior as well as other lights inside the house. Photo courtesy of the Genie Company.*

*Two-car garage with automatic door opener. Photo Courtest of the Genie Company.*

ramp by placing one or two steps at intervals on the run or length of the ramp. Another common safety break can be made in a long ramp, or in a flight of stairs, by building one or more long landings. Make the rise in the step(s) 6 inches or less, so a wheelchair can negotiate the rise.

The slope or grade of the ramp will depend on the lot and the relative position of the drive and/or street and the entry. You can even build a switchback into a ramp or set of stairs. A switchback is a run of steps or a ramp that rises in one direction, turns 180 degrees at a landing, and rises back to the top of the porch or entry landing. For use by wheelchairs, the recommended grade or slope is 1/12 (1 foot of rise for 12 feet of run, or less).

### Ramp Specifications

An exterior ramp can replace steps where necessary, making entrances much easier to negotiate for those who must use walking aids or wheelchairs. Ideally, all entrances in the house would be ramped, so that all occupants could exit through any door in an emergency. It is critical that at least one entrance have a ramp, so the wheelchair occupant can make an emergency exit unaided if necessary.

How much slope a wheelchair can negotiate depends on whether the wheelchair is powered or propelled by hand; and if propelled by hand, how much upper body strength the person retains. As a general guideline, ramps should have no more than a 1/12 slope, or 1 foot of rise for 12 feet of run. This would mean that a ramp that must rise 2 feet to the top of a porch must be 2 x 12 feet or 24 feet long. Ideally, of course, the more gentle the ramp slope, the better for the user.

The ramp must be 3½ feet to 4 feet wide; again, the wider the better. Although technically a wheelchair can travel on a 3-foot wide path, it is difficult to keep the chair on an absolutely straight course if the wheels are turned by hand, so a margin on each side is recommended. The ramp can be poured of concrete or built of wood; whatever material is used, the surface should be as slip-resistant as possible. Concrete is more expensive but lasts longer and is easier to maintain. If you will be building the ramp yourself, use pre-treated lumber and be sure to add handrails.

## PORCH

The porch should be large enough so that a wheelchair can change directions. The usual recommendation for a wheelchair turning radius is 5 feet, but more is better. Also useful at the main entry is a porch roof to shelter you from the weather while trying to open the door. A shelf at the side of the door large enough to accept an armload of packages is a welcome addition. If a shelf will cramp the entry, consider building a folding shelf that will fold against the house siding or against the porch railing. Another option would be to build a porch seat into the railing, a seat that could be used either while waiting or for a bench to hold packages. Opening the door can be made easier, with less fumbling in the dark, with locks that open to a number code.

## WALKING — AROUND THE EXTERIOR

All walk surfaces of concrete should be textured with a nylon bristle broom to produce a rough, slip-free finish on the surface. That goes for the porch and steps as well as walks and drives. Also available are concrete coating products that can be painted on surfaces such as steps, drives, or poolside concrete aprons to guard against accidents on wet, slippery concrete surfaces.

Plant low-growing shrubbery along porches or walks and keep limbs pruned so they do not overhang the walking surface. Dig grass from between cracks in walks and use an edger to cut back the turf along the walk or drive and preserve the full concrete walkway. Remove toys, garden and lawn tools, and leaves, as well as snow and ice from any walking surface, and keep steps clear of shopping brochures, newspapers, and other such clutter.

Concrete surfaces should be sealed at least once a year, in the fall, before really cold weather begins. A clear concrete sealant will protect and preserve the concrete against moisture entry and subsequent freeze damage, and it will aid water runoff and help keep steps, porches, and walks free of water and ice.

## LIGHTING

Outdoor and entry lighting becomes more crucial as physical problems compound. Poor lighting can cause frustrating delays while we search for keys at the door, and vision fails us. Toys or other objects carelessly left on the pathways may be an aggravation to a young, mobile person, but can be threatening or even deadly barriers for the elderly or infirm, to whom any fall can mean hospitalization and possibly surgery. Exterior and yard lighting can be a welcome safeguard if properly done.

### Lighting for Security

A major concern for the elderly and for us all is home security. Be sure your home's entrances, garage, and any outbuildings are adequately lit. It's also a good idea to light the corners of your house and any bushes or shrubbery. You don't usually need flood lights to illuminate your home's exterior properly. Low voltage outdoor lights placed around your home can be just as effective. These are 12 volt lights that are stepped down from 120 volt service via a transformer.

Photoelectric lights that switch on automatically at dusk can ease fears from prowlers or intruders. One of these is First Alert®'s Automatic Light Control. It fits into a standard light socket. The photocell automatically turns the light on at dusk and off at dawn.

One of the best multi-purpose outdoor lights available is the motion detector floodlight. These lights use infrared motion detectors in specific areas and are only activated when something moves in the monitored area. These lights that detect motion are triggered if any intruder comes near but can save energy by being off but alert through the night. Motion detectors are especially useful for illuminating driveways, walkways, and porches. The Solar Sentinel from Sunergy, Inc. is a solar-powered motion detector that is easy to install and inexpensive to operate. Sound-activated lights are available also. These come on if any noise above pre-screened background levels is detected.

The following are some manufacturers of motion detector lighting:

Chronar Corporation, Sunergy Inc.
P.O. Box 177
Princeton, NJ 08542
(800) CHRONAR

Consumer Group (Elcctripak)
P.O. Box 30489
Memphis, TN 38130-0489

First Alert®
BRK Electronics
780 McClure Road
Aurora, IL 60504-2495
(312) 851-7330

Intelectron
21021 Corsair Blvd.
Hayward, CA 94545
(415) 732-6790

TestRite Products Corporation
395 Allwood Road
Clifton, NJ 07012
(201) 773-9109

As mentioned, lights can be triggered by the

garage door opener to light a pathway in the dark, and remote control devices can be carried in pocket or purse to light the interior as you approach the darkened house.

Low-voltage yard lighting can be installed to mark a garden walkway, to delineate the boundaries of a deck or patio, or to outline a flower bed. If you decide to use floodlights, keep in mind that they should be pointed downward from the eaves or upward from the ground toward the house. Lights pointed away from the house can actually provide enough glare to hide an intruder.

For more information about lighting and safety, contact the National Lighting Bureau. This Bureau offers a free pamphlet entitled "Lighting and Security." It describes how proper outdoor lighting can deter burglars, improve safety, and provide other benefits. Another booklet offered is "Lighting for Safety and Security" ($5 a copy). Aimed primarily at businesses, this booklet is also useful for homeowners. These titles can be ordered from:

National Lighting Bureau
2101 L Street N.W., Suite 300
Washington, DC 20037
(202) 457-8437

## GARDENING

Limited mobility need not prevent a gardener from pursuing his hobby. Hydroponic gardening can be done in limited space and by those with limited mobility. Vegetables planted in deck or patio planting tubs or in window boxes can provide both fresh salads and hours of diversion. Scooter-type devices, available from garden catalogs or lawn and garden stores, let the user move about the garden rows while seated. One of these scooters, and many of the other items mentioned above, is available from:

Gardener's Supply
128 Intervale Road
Burlington, VT 05401
(802) 863-1700

For those who wish to garden on a grand scale, raised planting beds combined with intensive gardening can provide all the diversion and reward you could hope for. Build raised beds with wide seating ledges at chair or wheelchair levels for easy access. Build in wooden lockers for tool storage, and extend outdoor water faucets to the raised planting area, using easy-to-plumb plastic tubing and fittings. Pave a path, at least 4 feet wide, of concrete, to increase mobility around the perimeter of the raised bed.

CHECKLIST

# THE HOME'S EXTERIOR

❑ The lot for the barrier-free house should be located near public transportation, churches, shopping, and medical facilities.

❑ The lot should have little elevation (slope) or be terraced with ramps.

❑ Drives and walks should be wide enough to accommodate the needs of those in wheelchairs. Surfaces should be smooth, without joints or heavy textures that might trip up the infirm.

❑ Steps should be avoided, and ramps used wherever possible. Steps should be slip-proof and as wide as the walks or porches they connect.

❑ All approaches to the house and connected patios or decks should be well-lit, with focus lighting at steps and walking hazards. Motion detector lights and yard lights with automatic timers can aid home security.

❑ Automatic sprinklers for the lawn can eliminate the chore of moving hoses and sprinklers. Buried water supply lines also eliminate the tripping hazard of having garden hoses strewn about the walks and yard.

❑ Raised garden beds and hydroponic gardens let the less abled pursue garden hobbies while eliminating stooping and bending. Small-plot gardening helps retain the satisfaction one gets from gardening but can eliminate the need for extensive cultivation, weeding, and watering.

❑ Use fiberglass ground cloth in gardens or planting beds to let water through while discouraging weed growth.

❑ Ground covers such as cedar or redwood chips or bark add visual interest to the yard while reducing the need to water and weed. Mulch used on garden areas will also reduce yard work.

❑ Ask experts to test the lawn and bring it into proper pH balance to reduce the need for expensive chemical additives. Monitor the use of watering and fertilizers to keep the lawn in good health while reducing yard chores.

❑ Choose building materials for long life and low maintenance. Brick, stucco, and aluminum and vinyl sidings require little maintenance. Warp-free steel or fiberglass doors provide superior insulation, do not require an extra storm door, and are virtually maintenance-free.

❑ Build any decks or other additions to the house to match existing floor levels, with no steps to impede movement for the less abled.

# 2
# Entries, Stairs, and Halls

Entries, stairs, and halls pose the biggest problem when designing or remodeling an accessible home. This chapter discusses the importance of design for doors and doorways, floor coverings in these areas, stairways, lighting, and foyers and entryways.

## DOORS AND DOORWAYS

To be wheelchair accessible, all entry doors must be at least 3 feet wide, with double entry doors a plus. For exterior doors, beveled wood thresholds can be used or you can purchase beveled metal thresholds. Use weatherstripping around the door for a tight seal.

The typical door which is hinged on the side and swings in is the most difficult to handle for the disabled person. French doors, in which both doors must be opened for entry or exit are just as bad. Remove or replace such interior doors with folding or sliding doors.

### Knobs, Handles, and Locks

Rather than conventional knobs, doors should be opened and closed with lever handles. One of these, the Leveron®, can be installed over an existing doorknob. Made of a thermoplastic mate-

rial, it requires only one-third the force of metal lever hardware to operate. A "Hi-Glow" model is offered which remains visible in total darkness for several hours. The Leveron® is available from:

Lindustries, Inc.
21 Shady Hill Road
Weston, MA 02193
(617) 237-8177 or 235-5452

If changing to lever handles is impractical, foam-rubber door knob covers are available. These are inexpensive and provide a better gripping surface than slippery metal.

Numbered push-button locks eliminate fumbling with keys. Low, almost flush thresholds under doors ease the chore of entering over obstacles such as high threshold entries. Older homes may have triangular beveled thresholds on interior doors. These should all be removed. If you plan to sell the house later, mark each threshold with its location and store them in the garage or attic.

## ENTRYWAYS

Inside, it is best if the foyer is built at the same level as the main floor, not sunken or raised. One-level houses with no steps are the ideal plan for barrier-free living. Non-slip floor coverings are

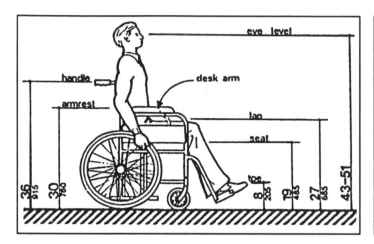

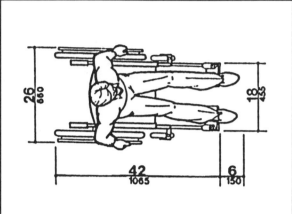

*Dimensions of adult-sized wheelchairs.*

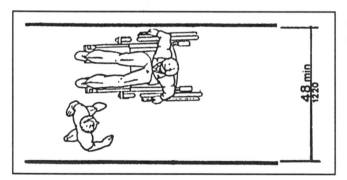

*Minimum passage width for one wheelchair and one ambulatory person.*

*Space needed for smooth U-turn in a wheelchair.*

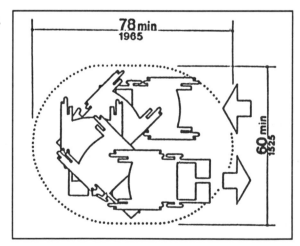

also required for safe footing. If carpet is used in the entry or foyer it should be a tightly-woven type with no loops or high nap to trip up unsteady feet or walking aids. If there is room in the foyer a bench is a handy aid so one can remove overshoes or rubbers while seated. The hall closet should have adjustable shelves and poles that can be set to accommodate a person who must be seated in a wheelchair.

Dimmer switches on entry lights permit the option of keeping light levels low for economy but increasing light levels for those who need more light to work by. Through-door viewers and even closed circuit security cameras at entry doors let occupants view visitors before deciding whether to permit them to enter. Deadbolt locks are high-security items at entry doors, but select deadbolts that do not interfere with easy exits.

## STAIRS

Statistics from the Consumer Product Safety Commission tell us that one in seven people will be injured and require hospitalization due to a stairway accident, some time in their lives. Truly barrier-free houses will have not stairs to contend with, but families may experience changes in member mobility. If you have a house with stairs and wish to make them safer, there are ways to do so.

First, check out stairway lighting. You must be able to see clearly to avoid stair accidents. Overhead lights at top and bottom stair landings are minimum requirements. Lighting can also be added in the risers between stairs, for unshadowed lighting on the steps themselves. Or light fixtures can be recessed into the walls that enclose the stairs.

Keep in mind that many code-approved standards are only guidelines and are not the optimum possible standards from a safety standpoint. Stair and hall widths of 3 feet are commonly code approved, but these minimum widths may prove inadequate for meeting special needs. For a person confined to a wheelchair, or with limited mobility, standard code measurements can be confining. Halls and stairways are not only easier to travel through if they are 4 feet wide, but moving furniture in or out becomes a much more agreeable task if you can fit it around corners.

By the same token, code requirements for stair risers and treads can be unacceptable for safety generally, especially so for those with limited mobility. Common code requirements for tread width dictate 9 inches, which is less than the length of most adult feet. This means that you cannot fit your entire foot on most stair treads. Carpeting the stairs can reduce usable tread width to 8 or even 7 inches, and this narrow tread invites injury from falling. Build stair treads that are at least 11 inches wide, so you can fit your entire foot on the tread for safety. By the same token, codes may permit a riser height — the distance between steps — of 8 inches, maximum. But this comparatively high step can cause a person to stub a toe on the riser. It is much better to limit riser height to 7 inches.

Remember, too, that carpeting the stairs reduces the usable tread width by the thickness of carpet and padding. Carpet can be warm and soft underfoot, and can help noiseproof the stairs to sleeping areas. But carpet can also be a safety hazard for those who are unsteady on foot. If you insist on carpeting for stairs, use only tightly-woven carpet with no loops or high nap to tangle with feet and cause a fall. For padding, insist on ¼ - inch thick commercial (dense) padding to minimize falling caused by reduced tread width. Avoid using carpets that have textures or patterns; they may make steps hard to see because they present a continuous background.

### Handrails

Handrails for stairs, to be truly useful, should be

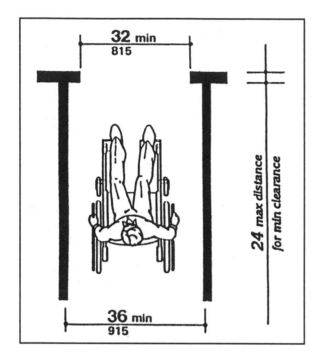

*Minimum clear width for single wheelchair.*

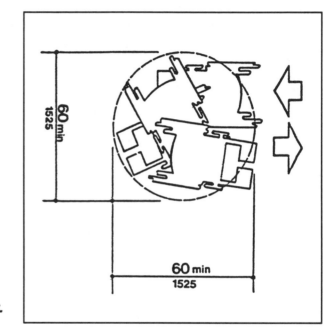

*Wheelchair turning space — 60-inch diameter.*

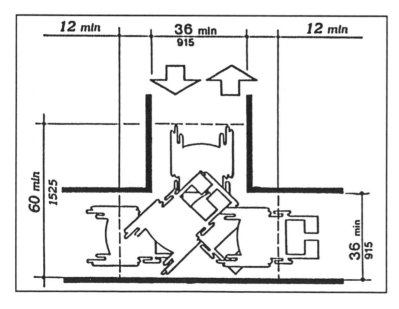

*Wheelchair turning space — T-shaped space for 180° turns.*

able to support the weight of an adult without breaking. If you inspect the handrails in your own home you may find the railing too poorly fastened (with short screws), too thick to grip, or too weak to support your weight in an emergency. For home safety, whatever your physical capabilities, be sure the handrails are of proper size and properly installed.

Handrails often are installed at 32 inches above the stair treads, but 36 inches is a better height for support in the event of a fall. The handrail should be secured with brackets, screwed into wall studs with screws no less that 1½ inches long for wallboard, 2 inches long minimum if the screw passes through plaster. Unscrew existing screws and check to be sure that they are tight, that they are driven into studs, not just into plaster lath, and that you have wall brackets spaced at 4-foot intervals. The wood rail should be a standard handrail — 1½ inches in diameter. This diameter is large enough to provide good handrail strength, but small enough so that you can clasp fingers and thumb completely around the rail, and therefore have a good grip.

Pull hard upon the handrail to check that it is securely fastened to the wall, not loose or wiggly. If the handrail is set on top of stair balusters, check the balusters to be sure they are not loose.

Finally, the end of the handrail should curve inward at the bottom and top steps, to signal that you are at the end of the stair run. Handrails that end too abruptly leave you wondering where the stairs end and can present a real hazard to the occupant.

## Lifts

For those who cannot negotiate stairs at all, stair way lifts that travel on a rail are available. A fold-up seat permits occupants to fold the seat out of the way when the stairs are used by foot travelers, and to fold the seat down when a passenger wishes to ride the lift. To find a dealer for these stairway lifts, check the Appendix in the back of this book or look in the Yellow Pages under "Elevators — Sales and Service."

## HALLS

As mentioned earlier, all passageways in a home should be a minimum of 4 feet wide. Codes will accept 3-foot wide halls, a minimum that was adapted for postwar housing, when one conserved floor space by building at minimum room sizes. But anyone who has ever tried to negotiate a stairway or hall while moving a queen- or king-sized mattress knows that 3 feet is hardly the desirable width for passage.

A wheelchair occupant can pass through a hall that is 3 feet wide. But this narrow width will not permit a wheelchair to turn from the hall into a room, through a 32-inch wide door. You can remove the narrow 32-inch door and replace it with a 3-foot wide door to let a wheelchair make the turn from the hall through the door. Much better, however, is to build the hallway at least 4 feet wide, and to keep hall lengths at the very minimum length, to reduce barriers as much as possible.

Floor covering in a hall can be vinyl, hardwood, or tightly woven carpet. Remember that carpet and padding thickness can become a real problem to those who are infirm or use a wheelchair. Choose floor covering carefully for high-traffic areas such as halls.

CHECKLIST

# ENTRIES, STAIRS, AND HALLS

❏ All doors should be 3-0 (36 inches) wide to provide maximum freedom of passage for wheelchairs.

❏ Consider using keyed push-button entry locks to avoid fumbling with house keys.

❏ Lever-type door handles are easier to operate than are the more common round door knobs. Round knobs can be slippery and hard to turn if gripping strength is limited.

❏ Avoid using thumb-latch entry doors. These are difficult to operate for those with arthritic hands or loss of hand strength.

❏ Provide good lighting at entry doors to aid those with reduced vision.

❏ Build a shelf by the entry door so you have a place to put packages while you negotiate the entry. The shelf can be one that folds away when not in use.

❏ Keep shrubs and trees near entries well trimmed so that they do not provide a hiding place for intruders.

❏ Garage doors should have automatic lights and openers so that nighttime entry is easier and safer. Some garage door openers have multiple functions, so you can also operate lights inside the house to light your path on entry.

❏ Do not block steps or porches with potted plants or other objects that might be tripped over in the dark.

❏ Provide secure handrails at any exterior steps and porches. Keep concrete slabs sealed to aid water runoff and avoid having ice or puddles forming on steps, walks, or drives.

❏ Equip entry doors with peepholes or with closed-circuit video, so visitors can be identified before the door is opened.

❏ Build or remodel hallways so they are 4 feet wide.

❏ Do not carpet stairs. Carpet can cause tripping and reduces width of steps. Bare wood, or wood covered with non-slip vinyl covers, is safer underfoot. If you must carpet, choose a low-pile carpet backed by a commercial ¼-inch pad.

❏ Check stair rails to be sure they are properly secured and will not come loose in case of a fall. Most rails are secured with too-small screws that will fail if a person's falling weight is upon them.

☐ Handrails should not be varnished and should be small enough in diameter that the average-sized hand can encircle them for a secure grip.

# 3
# The Bathroom

It should come as no surprise that the bathroom is the most dangerous room in the house. When you consider that we combine steam, water, electricity, and slippery — even when dry — surfaces in the room, then adorn the walls with protruding tub spouts and faucet handles to give us one more blow on the way down, you can see the potential for disaster. Yet an entire array of safety products is out there and can be installed at little cost, even as retrofits, to help us through our daily rituals.

## ACCESS

The first challenge for the wheelchair occupant is to get into the bathroom. Bathroom doors are often a minimal 2'-6" wide (known as 2-6). In fact, the 2-6 door opening, nominally 30 inches wide, is a scant 27 inches wide when we deduct the width of jambs and stops. A person in a wheelchair cannot turn from a 3-foot wide hallway into a 27-inch wide door. The narrow door should be removed, and a 3-0 or 36-inch wide door installed in its place. Also, the bathroom door should swing outward, into the hall, rather than swinging into the bathroom as is usual. The door takes up space in the bathroom if it swings inward.

Another option is to install a sliding or pocket door to the bathroom. Pocket doors slide into a pocket in the wall, rather than swinging into a room or a hall, so the door is not taking up any space. They are usually used in mobile homes or small apartments where space is at a premium, but are a real spacesaver in any house.

Bathrooms built prior to the 1960s were commonly shoehorn affairs, built 5 feet wide (the width of a standard bathtub) and usually 7 feet long. This 5 x 7 foot configuration was the minimum size allowed under FHA and GI building codes, and millions of homes have that limited area. Obviously, if you install a bathtub, lavatory, and toilet in that small space, then swing a door into the space left, you have no room to move into the space with a wheelchair and still negotiate movement between the chair and the tub or the toilet. If your house has such a small bathroom, it would be well to consider expanding the room into an adjoining bedroom space or to tear out linen or other closets and include the gained space in a revised bathroom. To be useful to a wheelchair occupant, the bathroom must have an open 5-foot turning radius for the chair to maneuver and turn.

Planning the bathroom layout so that a telephone can be reached from either the toilet or shower stall can also be a great convenience for any family member. Running with wet feet across a wet, slippery floor to answer a telephone call can be inviting disaster.

*Pedestal sink permits access with leg room underneath. Raised platform around the tub provides seating for transfer from wheelchair to tub. Aqualine fixtures from Eljer. Photo courtesy of Eljer Co.*

*Required clear knee space at lavatories (ANSI and UFAS).*

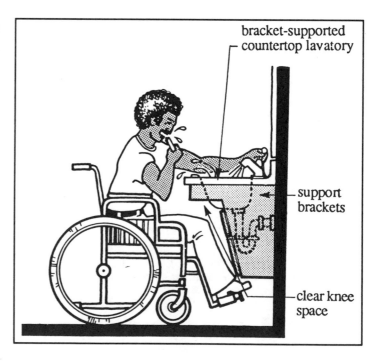

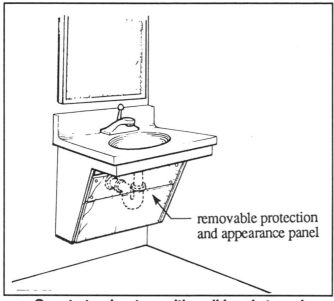

Countertop lavatory with wall brackets and protective panel.

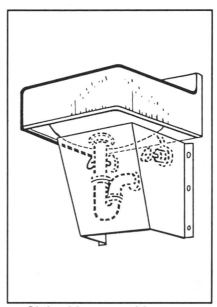

Sink with removable cover for pipe protection.

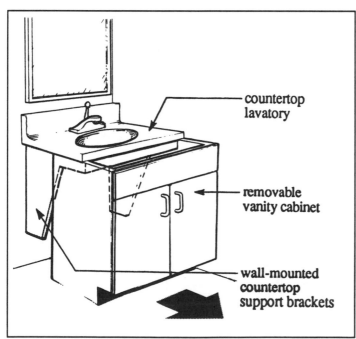

countertop lavatory

removable vanity cabinet

wall-mounted countertop support brackets

Removing vanity cabinet to expose knee space.

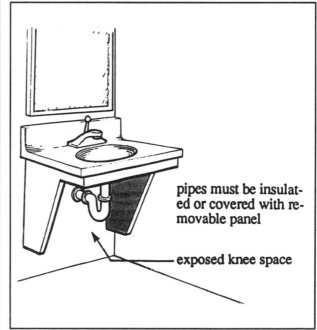

removable protection and appearance panel

pipes must be insulated or covered with removable panel

exposed knee space

Exposed knee space under bracket-supported, countertop lavatory.

*Low-flow Wellworth Lite™ toilet uses only one-third as much water as older toilets, reducing utility bills. Photo courtesy of Kohler Co.*

*Adjustable guard rails fit around toilet and provide lifting point for those who have limited mobility. Photo courtesy of Frohock-Stewart, Inc.*

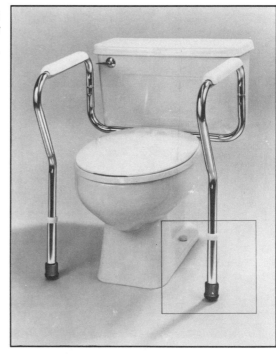

## FLOORING

Check out flooring options to find one that is slip-resistant. Don't overlook materials that are normally designed for hospital or institutional use: you are not limited to using floor covering that is offered to the consumer. Cork, non-slip vinyls, and ceramic tiles with textured surfaces can provide better footing to the unsteady.

## LAVATORY AND CABINETS

Rather than having the familiar vanity cabinet with the lavatory sink recessed into the cabinet countertop, consider using a wall-hung lavatory, which will permit a wheelchair occupant to have leg space beneath the sink. Be sure the wall-hung lavatory is properly secured to the wall.

Small wall-hung cabinets can be installed on one or both sides of the lavatory, as space and need permit. Mirrors in the bath should be mounted so a person seated at wheelchair height can easily see to shave or apply makeup. The bottom of the mirror should be no higher than 36 inches from the floor. The medicine chest should be within easy reach and have adjustable shelves. The tilt-out type chest may be the best choice. Mount the medicine chest next to, rather than over, the sink. Soap dishes and toothbrush holders should be within reach, mounted no more than 42 inches above the floor.

## LIGHTING

Theater or strip lighting may be mounted above and on both sides of the mirror or on the sides only. Keep in mind that a person who is eighty years old may require up to three times as high a light-intensity level as a teenager, because of diminished eyesight. It is critical that high light levels be maintained at any location where people take medicine, to ensure against any mistakes in medication due to misread directions or taking the wrong medicine or the wrong dosage. Be sure to place an electrical outlet (ground fault circuit interrupter -type) near the sink.

## TOILETS

Wall-hung toilets can also be useful, as these have no floor pedestal to interfere with foot or leg movement. The wall-hung toilet may also be mounted so the toilet seat is at the same level as a wheelchair seat, for ease of movement between the two. For floor-mounted toilets there are extenders that can be fastened to the toilet (replacing the seat) to raise the seating level, or the toilet can be permanently mounted on a pedestal to bring it up to wheelchair height. Grab bars mounted to the walls, or bars that can be installed as floor-mounts, can be useful aids for those with limited mobility.

## BATHTUBS AND SHOWERS

Bathtubs or combination bathtub and shower units are now available for barrier-free installations. The molded fiberglass units feature ease of entry and built-in or foldup seating that can be put in place for family members who need assistance, but moved or folded away for more mobile people. Placement and strength of the grab bars meet ANSI (American National Standards Institute) recommendations, as does location of seating and soap dishes. Shower doors such as the TUB-MASTER provide seals at sides and floor so barrier-free shower stalls can be used without a curb at the floor. The wheelchair must only roll over a low vinyl threshold to gain admission to the shower stall.

Because home utility bills are the foremost concern for those on a fixed or limited income,

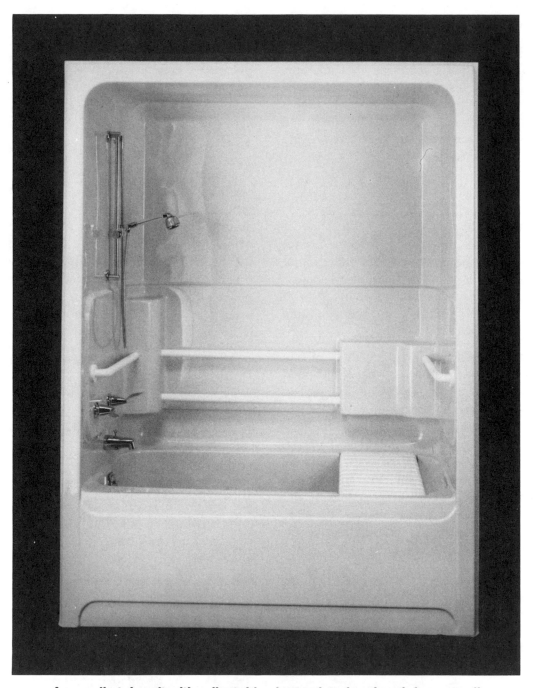

*An acrylic tub unit with adjustable shower head and grab bars on all three sides. Built-in seating can be either integral or fold-up. Faucet handles are large, flat levers. Photo courtesy of Kohler Co.*

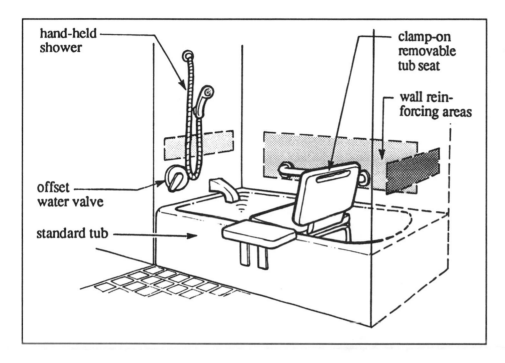

hand-held shower

offset water valve

standard tub

clamp-on removable tub seat

wall rein-forcing areas

*Standard bathtub with removable seat.*

*Standard bathtub with built-in seat.*

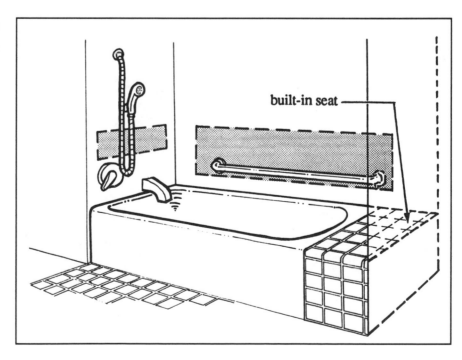

built-in seat

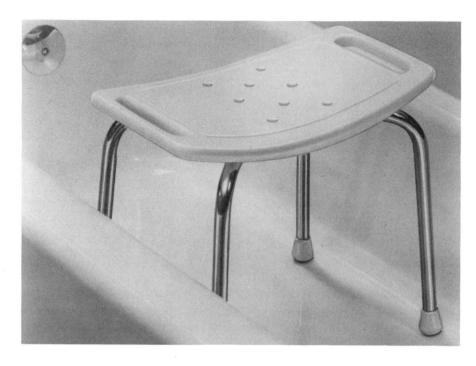

*For those who cannot sit down in a bathtub, a bath bench offers in-tub seating while bathing. Photo courtesy of Frohock-Stewart, Inc.*

*This bath bench comes with a back rest for those who need more back support. Photo courtesy of Frohock-Stewart, Inc.*

consider installing water-saving bathroom fixtures such as the Wellworth Lite™ by Kohler. Reducing home water consumption by half is an accessible goal, if you replace the standard toilet that uses 5 to 7 gallons per flush with the watersaver units that use only 1.5 gallons per flush. Combine this with low-flow shower heads that cut water consumption by half or more, and you have accomplished real savings.

## FAUCETS AND CONTROLS

To be considered for barrier-free installation, water faucets and controls must be easy to operate, must be water-saving, and must have anti-scald controls.

For ease of operation, install single-lever faucets at all sinks. These offer both temperature and volume control in one unit, with one hand. Large levers not only offer easier control for those with diminished hand strength, they also can be manipulated with a push of the hand or the elbow. Ceramic disc cartridge construction is a guarantee of low-maintenance operation, another concern for those who may be unable to manage maintenance chores themselves.

In addition to controlling water flow and temperature, barrier-free lavatory and shower faucets provide flexible, movable heads. The flexible extension shower heads permit you to control the position and direction of the shower head so you can bathe while sitting. The extension lavatory faucet is useful in permitting you to shampoo from a seated position.

## OTHER CONSIDERATIONS

### Grab Bars

Grab bars at tub and toilet, and inside the shower stall, would likely prevent tens of thousands of falls in the U.S. annually. New shower stalls or tubs may have grab bars molded into the unit, along with soap dishes at convenient height for bath or shower use. A soap caddy, hung over the shower head, can hold shampoo, soap, or washcloths at a convenient level so the bather is not moving or stretching outside the unit to reach needed items.

If your bathroom has no grab bars, there are many styles to choose from — bars that can be attached to any wall. It is important, however, to install the bars using screws large and long enough to support the weight of a falling person. These mounting screws should always be driven into the wood framing in the walls, not secured with plastic screw plugs or driven into lath or plaster only. Only screws that are driven into framing members are strong enough to support a person's weight.

### Laundry and Clothes Chute

Build a clothes chute in the bath to make it easy to transfer clothes or bath towels to the laundry. The clothes chute can be a through-the-wall door with a clothes hamper on the laundry side. The laundry in the barrier-free house should be on the main floor, not stuck away in an inaccessible basement. Even better, install spacesaver or stackable laundry equipment in the bathroom for the easiest access.

Provide as much storage at easy-to-reach levels as possible. Consider including narrow shelves and wall-mounted coated wire baskets.

### Ventilation

A bathroom should have an exterior window if possible, because the best dehumidifier and air freshener is outdoor air. The bathroom should also have an exhaust vent fan to move moisture outdoors during cold weather. Check out the types of windows available and make sure they are easy

*Low flexible-vinyl threshold on shower door eliminates the curb barrier common on most shower stalls. A wheelchair rolls effortlessly over the low threshold. Photo courtesy of Tub-Master Corp.*

*Barrier-free shower doors provide watertight seal at sides and bottom and permit wheelchair entry. Photo courtesy of Tub-Master Corp.*

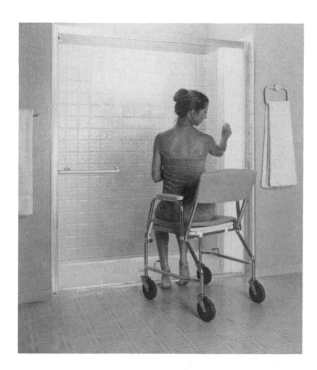

*Barrier-free shower unit is 42" x 36", has handle on water control plus shower control that can be hand-held. Grab bars and fold-away seating are useful for those with limited mobility. Photo courtesy of Kohler Co.*

*This shower seat provides safe support for those who need it but can be folded away for others. Photo courtesy of Kohler Co.*

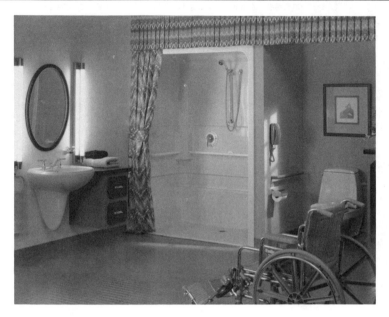

*This bathroom features Kohler's Freewill™ line of barrier-free units including curb-less acrylic shower stall with built-in grab bars and adjustable shower head. Wall-hung lavatory and toilet units can be set at any height to accommodate the users; lavatory also allows wheelchair occupant leg room under the lavatory. Mirror is hung lower than usual for convenient use while seated. Lights on sides of mirror provide higher light intensity than ordinary incandescent bulbs. Telephone is easily accessible from toilet or shower. Photo courtesy of Kohler Co.*

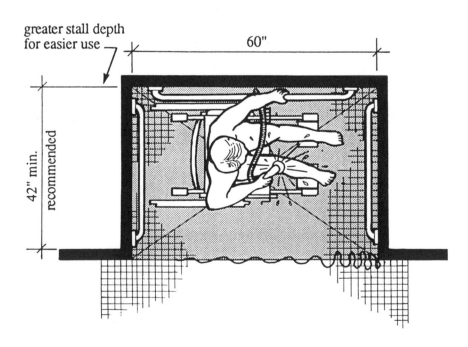

*Preferred deeper roll-in shower.*

to operate. Skylight windows are available with remote control openers that use push-button operation. Consider casement windows that have crank or lever openers that will ensure ease of operation.

## ADD-ON AIDS

There are a number of things you can do to make existing bathrooms barrier-free. If you are not building new or remodeling, the bath and shower units with built-in support features are not for your consideration. But you can add flexible shower heads and lever-type faucets to make bathing easier. Toilet extensions can replace the toilet seat to aid those who have trouble sitting lower. Grab bars that fit on walls, bathtub, or toilet can be added in any bathroom. Bath benches can be placed in tubs or showers to ease movement between tub and wheelchair or walker. Non-slip floor covering or bath mats can replace slippery surfaces.

Check with electrical stores for oversized light switches. Some switches require only a touch; some have oversized plates. For those who have to get up at night, install a bathroom light switch that is lighted so it is easy to find in the dark.

Bathroom hardware can be removed and replaced with hardware that is more user-friendly. On vanity cabinets, for example, it is simple and inexpensive to remove round pull knobs and replace them with D-type hardware pulls that are easier to grasp. Lever attachments that can be screwed onto round door knobs make room entry easier.

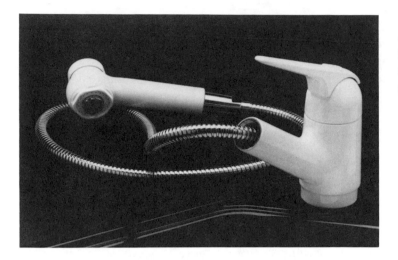

*The KWCvita faucet features built-in anti-scald controls for safety, plus flow controls for water conservation. The 6-inch U-lever can be controlled with arm or elbow if necessary. Photo courtesy of Western States Mfg. Corp.*

*Grohmix™ Thermostat/Pressure Balance Valve permits user to choose the temperature for bath or shower and maintain the temperature to within one degree. The valve combines safety and comfort for bathing physically impaired persons or children. Photo courtesy of Grohe America.*

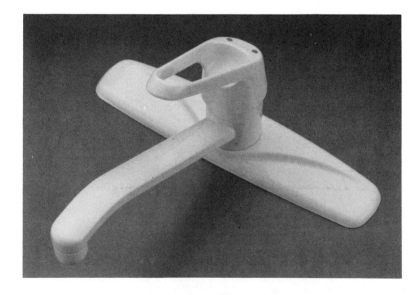

*Loop-handle faucet is easy to operate and controls both water volume and temperature. Photo courtesy of Eljer Co.*

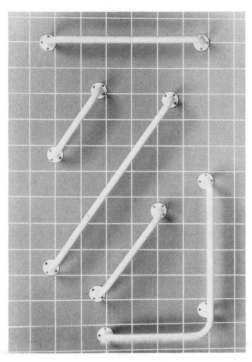

Grip rail is shaped to provide horizontal support at two height levels with one vertical bar. It can be attached to any bathtub. Courtesy of Frohock-Stewart, Inc.

Grab bars with soft vinyl finish. Photo courtesy of Frohock-Stewart, Inc.

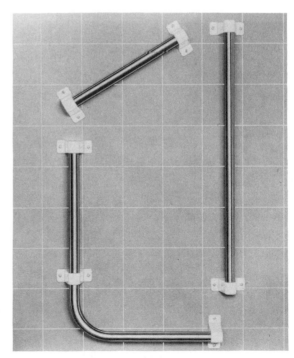

Straight or angled chrome-finish grab bars can be installed by the toilet or in the bath or shower. Photo courtesy of Frohock-Stewart, Inc.

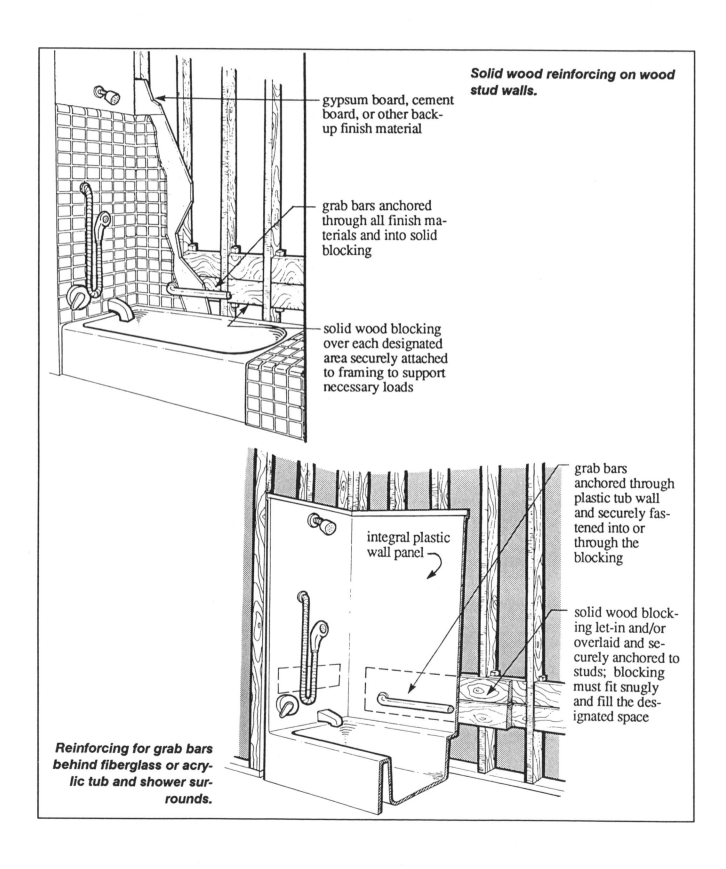

*Solid wood reinforcing on wood stud walls.*

gypsum board, cement board, or other back-up finish material

grab bars anchored through all finish materials and into solid blocking

solid wood blocking over each designated area securely attached to framing to support necessary loads

grab bars anchored through plastic tub wall and securely fastened into or through the blocking

integral plastic wall panel

solid wood blocking let-in and/or overlaid and securely anchored to studs; blocking must fit snugly and fill the designated space

*Reinforcing for grab bars behind fiberglass or acrylic tub and shower surrounds.*

## CHECKLIST
# THE BATHROOM

❏ The bathroom door should be wide enough to permit wheelchair entry. A 32-inch wide door from a wide hall is acceptable, but a 3-0 (36 inch) door is better.

❏ The bathroom floor plan should be large enough to permit a wheelchair to turn inside.

❏ Lavatories and toilets can be wall-mounted, which permits them to be positioned for wheelchair accessibility.

❏ Allow space beneath the lavatory sink for the wheelchair to approach. Consider having a wall-mounted countertop with an abbreviated vanity or no vanity cabinet underneath.

❏ Hang mirrors low enough to be used by the seated person.

❏ Provide enhanced lighting for those with reduced vision. Light should be bright enough to read prescription labels to avoid taking the wrong medicine or wrong dosage.

❏ Drawer pulls and round door knobs on vanities should be D-shaped for better gripping.

❏ Install non-slip flooring. Ceramic tile flooring can be perfectly safe if you choose the type used in hospitals and laboratories. These offer the resistance to dirt and stains, easy cleaning, and low maintenance normally associated with ceramic tile floors, with good traction underfoot.

❏ If building a new home, check out the barrier-free tubs and showers offered (see chapter illustrations).

❏ Bars and seats to aid tub entry are available at hospital supply stores (see Yellow Pages, "Hospital Equipment & Supplies").

❏ Install grab bars for safety wherever the less abled must stand and to aid entry and exit in bathtubs or shower stalls. Be sure grab bars are well anchored, with screws into wood framing, not just into plaster or drywall.

❏ Provide plenty of ventilation so that steam and moisture do not collect and make fixtures or floor slippery.

❏ If building new or remodeling, have the plumber offset water faucets and shower controls so they are near the front edge of the tub or shower stall, rather than having them centered over the tub.

❑ If space permits, install stackable laundry equipment in an alcove or closet in the bathroom. This eases laundry chores by keeping the laundry area central to the bath.

❑ Turn water heater thermostat down to prevent accidental scalding.

❑ Faucets should have lever handles for easy control of water temperature and flow.

❑ Install the medicine cabinet so it is not centered over the sink but allows easy access for a wheelchair occupant.

# 4
# The Kitchen

The kitchen and the bathroom are the most used, and the most remodeled, rooms in the house. They are also the only two rooms in which all the building trades are included: plumbing, wiring, cabinetry, and ceramic tile — all are found in these two rooms. In addition, the kitchen plan must include provisions for fitting in all the appliances for food storage, preparation, and disposal, so the kitchen is the most important room when planning to make a house barrier-free.

One thing to keep in mind is that many factors in a house, including the height of electrical outlets and switches, countertop height, and cabinet placement, are all compromises. There is no very good reason to make all countertops 36 inches from the floor. This really pleases only those of average height, while short people still stretch and tall people still stoop to work at the countertop. A better solution is to build countertops at varying levels so that people of all ages, sizes, and degrees of physical capability can find a workable level somewhere in the kitchen. Countertops near cooktops can be set for work height that will accommodate a standing person, because the user does not usually sit by a cooktop while it is operating. Countertops at desks, or where food is prepared, can be placed at heights to accommodate a person who cannot stand for long periods or is confined to a wheelchair. An increasing number of appliance manufacturers, cabinet makers, and building or remodeling contractors can provide aid or information on meeting any specific needs.

## CABINETS

The basic reason that cabinets and countertops are placed as they are is that the heights are a compromise to aid resale. If your cabinets are set at very low levels, to accommodate a housekeeper in a wheelchair, the kitchen will be unsalable to much of the buying public. One solution is to build cabinets and countertops at varying heights, assuming the kitchen is large enough to have multiple work surfaces. This is probably best, because it will not affect resale value. Then again, the less able person may buy or remodel a house so it is custom-built for that person's needs, and that person will be content to stay put in the specially-designed house for many years. The cost of remodeling the kitchen becomes less of a factor after that period of time. The ideal solution is to build a house — and kitchen — that simply removes most of the barriers that can be a deterrent to *any* person who lives in the house.

### Adjustable-height Cabinets

At the 1990 Builders Show in Atlanta, Georgia,

*This barrier-free kitchen, designed by Whirlpool and Home magazine editors, has work surfaces set at varying heights for use by all family members. Appliances are positioned for easy access; open plan reduces traffic jams while providing easy wheelchair access. Photo courtesy of Whirlpool Corp.*

*Low wall oven, swing-up mixer shelf, and lighted baking center provide easy access for a handicapped or elderly person. Photo courtesy of Whirlpool Corp.*

*This kitchen includes a second, under-counter microwave oven and pull-out work surface with a center cutout to hold a mixing bowl. Note front controls and staggered burners in the cooktop. Photo courtesy of Whirlpool Corp.*

*pull-out work surface*

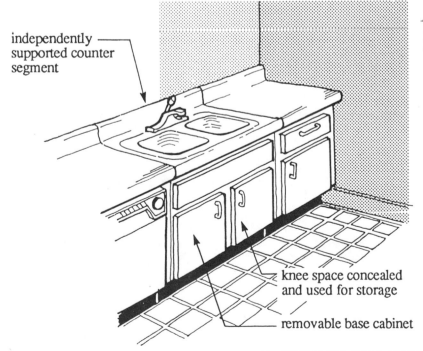

independently supported counter segment

**_Removable modified standard base cabinet in knee space._**

knee space concealed and used for storage

removable base cabinet

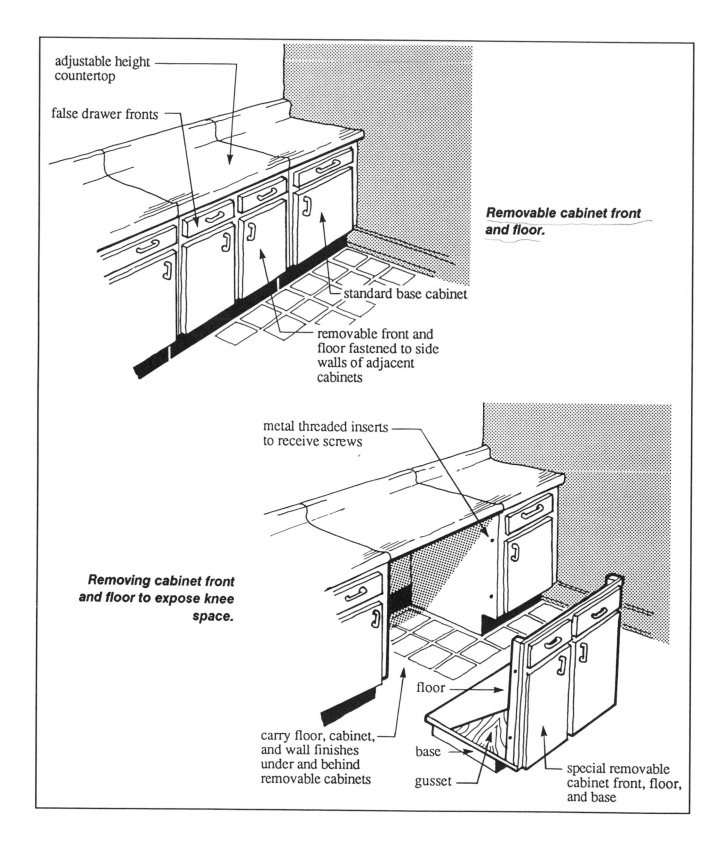

adjustable height countertop

false drawer fronts

**Removable cabinet front and floor.**

standard base cabinet

removable front and floor fastened to side walls of adjacent cabinets

metal threaded inserts to receive screws

**Removing cabinet front and floor to expose knee space.**

carry floor, cabinet, and wall finishes under and behind removable cabinets

floor

base

gusset

special removable cabinet front, floor, and base

one manufacturer exhibited motorized, height adjustable cabinets. Counters, cabinets, sinks, and cooktops are all motorized so they can be height adjusted at the touch of a switch.

The person who must work from a seated position can raise sink or countertop to position a wheelchair underneath, can lower upper cabinets to reach cooking or eating utensils, and can cook in a low-level, wall-mounted oven. Or multiple users can adjust one work surface for a standing worker and lower a sink for a seated person to wash dishes or clean countertops. Such motorized components are obviously more expensive than cabinets that are simply screwed to the wall, but the special cabinetry can be taken out and moved with the person who needs it, in case of a house sale. The company offering this adjustable cabinet system is:

Granberg Superior Systems Inc.
1221 State Street, Suite 24
Santa Barbara, CA 93103
(805) 965-0998

### Cabinet Configurations

One can lower upper cabinet heights to make them more easily reachable, but consider first the potential loss of countertop usability if you lower upper cabinets too much. It is easier to re-configure lower cabinets to hold dishes, cups, and glasses that are usually placed in upper cabinets, so they can be reached by a seated person. When planning the kitchen, consider how many cooking and cleaning chores will be done by the seated person. Often, changing the makeup of a lower cabinet, or adding one lower cabinet, can put everything needed within reach of any family member.

Cabinets do not need to be installed in an unbroken wall, thereby presenting an obstacle to the person in a wheelchair. A truly barrier-free kitchen would have no under-sink cabinet, because so much of food cleaning and preparation is done at the sink. An option would be to include a cabinet front on the undersink area, but make the front so it can be removed if it becomes a barrier. By the same token, lower cabinets are very rarely built in place in these days of prefabrication, and a countertop could be supported by key base units, with intermediate cabinets not attached to the countertop above but simply held in place with screws that could be backed out and the cabinet module pulled out, to gain leg space for the seated worker. In older cabinetry, unused built-in bread boards can have a hole cut in them, so a mixing bowl can be inserted and securely held while a person is using it.

If you are installing new cabinets, look for those that have magnetic door catches. These are opened simply by pushing and releasing the door, so no amount of hand strength or dexterity is needed. If cabinets must have pulls, choose hardware with D-shaped handles that can be easily gripped. Most difficult to grip are the round knobs in brass or glass that are both small and slippery, and thus are difficult to pull for those with diminished hand strength. It is both a simple and an inexpensive job to remove knob-type door or drawer pulls and replace them with D-type handles.

Cabinet shelves should be narrow enough to reach the back of the shelves easily — 8 to 10 inches deep for storage.

## COOKTOPS AND OVENS

A cooktop and wall-mounted oven are a better choice than a floor-standing range for barrier-free living. If a wall-mounted oven is chosen, it should not be placed above the range. The oven can be mounted lower so the cook does not have to stoop or bend to inspect cooking food, or to remove hot pans from the oven. Choose a self-cleaning oven for easy maintenance.

Most experts recommend using all electric appliances, for several reasons. First, there are no

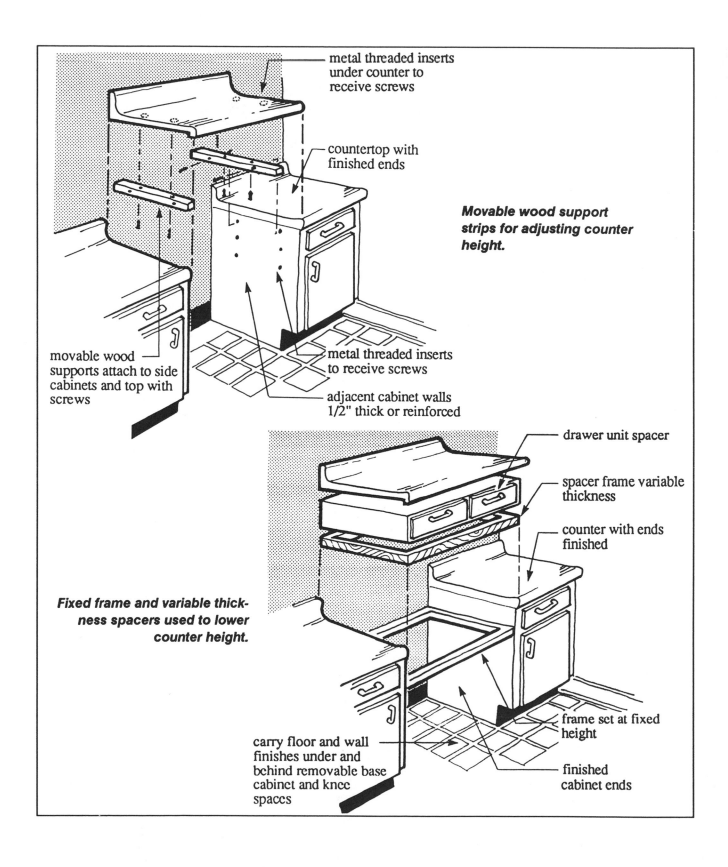

metal threaded inserts
under counter to
receive screws

countertop with
finished ends

*Movable wood support
strips for adjusting counter
height.*

movable wood
supports attach to side
cabinets and top with
screws

metal threaded inserts
to receive screws

adjacent cabinet walls
1/2" thick or reinforced

drawer unit spacer

spacer frame variable
thickness

counter with ends
finished

*Fixed frame and variable thick-
ness spacers used to lower
counter height.*

frame set at fixed
height

carry floor and wall
finishes under and
behind removable base
cabinet and knee
spaces

finished
cabinet ends

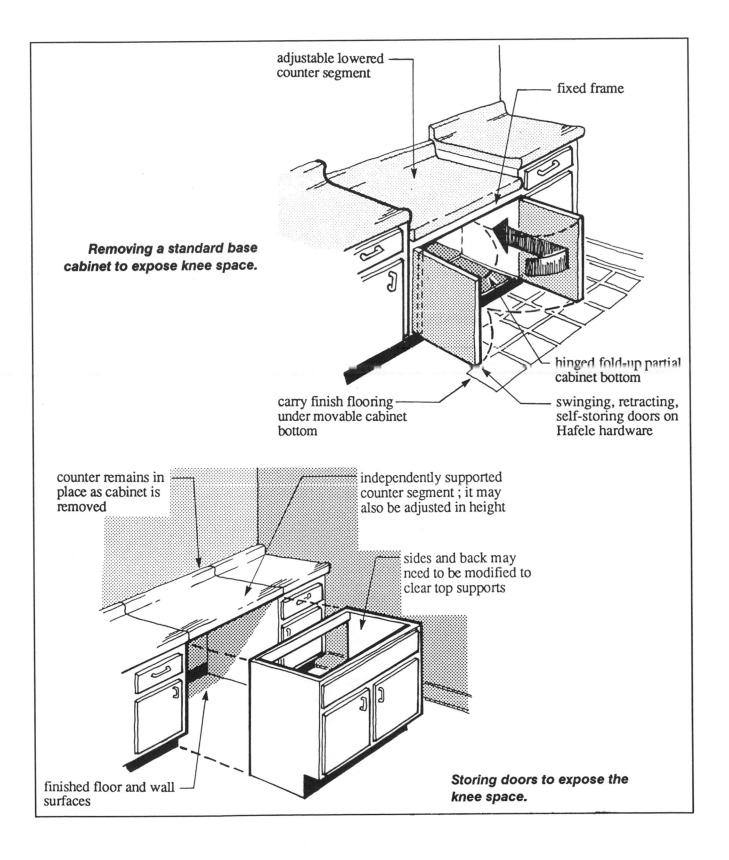

adjustable lowered counter segment

fixed frame

**Removing a standard base cabinet to expose knee space.**

hinged fold-up partial cabinet bottom

carry finish flooring under movable cabinet bottom

swinging, retracting, self-storing doors on Hafele hardware

counter remains in place as cabinet is removed

independently supported counter segment ; it may also be adjusted in height

sides and back may need to be modified to clear top supports

finished floor and wall surfaces

**Storing doors to expose the knee space.**

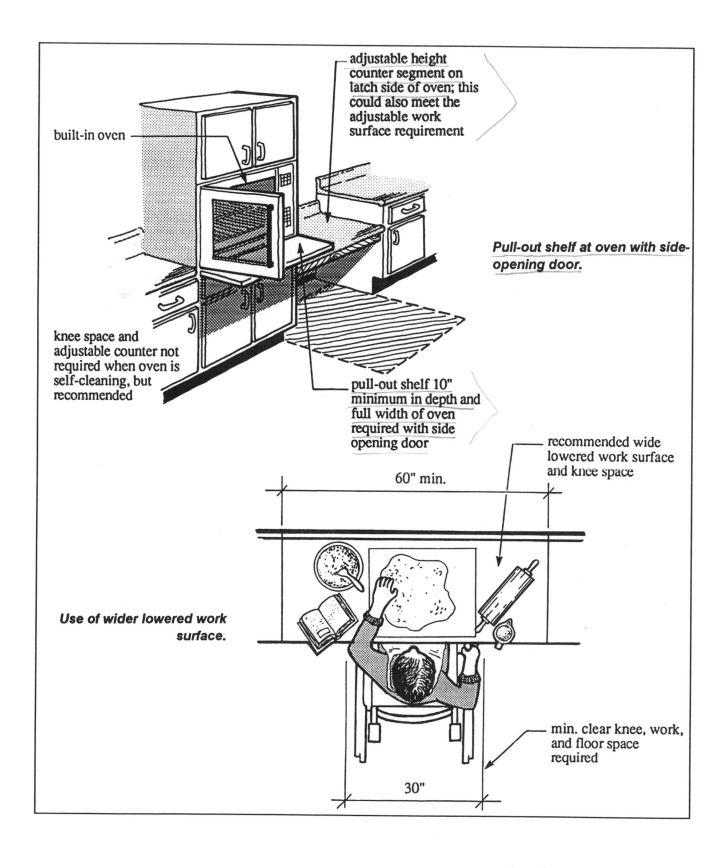

built-in oven

adjustable height counter segment on latch side of oven; this could also meet the adjustable work surface requirement

**Pull-out shelf at oven with side-opening door.**

knee space and adjustable counter not required when oven is self-cleaning, but recommended

pull-out shelf 10" minimum in depth and full width of oven required with side opening door

recommended wide lowered work surface and knee space

60" min.

**Use of wider lowered work surface.**

min. clear knee, work, and floor space required

30"

products of combustion such as carbon monoxide when using electrical appliances. This is increasingly important as we "tighten up" our houses for energy conservation. Next, people who have an impaired sense of smell will not be able to detect a gas leak.

The cooktop should have its controls on the front or side rather than the top, so a seated person will not have to reach across a hot burner to adjust the controls. Also, the burners should be staggered, not in line where the user must reach over a hot front burner to get at a rear burner.

By all means, barrier-free kitchens must have one or more microwave ovens. The microwave ovens produce no combustion gases, cook quickly, and are both safer and cheaper to operate for most cooking chores. To be accessible the microwave must be set on a countertop or installed in base cabinets, not positioned high on a wall or shelf.

Keep in mind that appliance companies such as Whirlpool Corp. offer optional Braille controls and instruction on cooking and other appliances.

## REFRIGERATOR

The side-by-side refrigerator is the hands-down winner for family accessibility. The lower shelves of both the refrigerator and the freezer can be stocked for the person who cannot reach the upper shelves.

Refrigerators with through-the-door dispensers provide no-fuss access to ice cubes and water. Large door shelves can hold gallon-sized milk containers or other beverages, while crisper bins keep fruits and vegetables at hand.

If you opt for a separate freezer, choose the upright type rather than the chest type. The upright freezer will take up less floor space, and the contents can readily be seen and reached by a wheelchair user.

## HOT WATER DISPENSERS

Hot water dispensers are very useful in any busy household but can combine both convenience and safety for those who might burn themselves while heating water with a kettle or reaching hot water from a microwave oven. The hot water dispenser can run the full range in prices: from $130 for KitchenAid's Instant-Hot to around $200 for Broan's Model HWD-5D, which has a gooseneck spout. All models offer a hot water flow of forty to sixty cups per hour, at a temperature of 190 degrees.

The water dispensers permit the user to make instant coffee, tea, hot chocolate, instant soup, or breakfast food in a jiffy and with the utmost ease and safety.

Hot water dispensers include a heating element plus thermostat, an electric cord which is plugged into a grounded under-sink receptacle, and a copper water supply tube with a saddle valve. They are easy to install yourself, with the major project installing the under-sink electrical receptacle.

The saddle valve must be mounted on the cold water supply pipe. Just connect the saddle valve to the supply tube, then bolt the two halves of the saddle valve to the water supply pipe.

Turn the self-piercing mechanism on the valve all the way in, to pierce the water pipe, then turn it back out so water can flow up to the heater. The spout can be located through the fourth hole in the sink or in a 1⅜-inch hole drilled through the countertop.

## OTHER APPLIANCES

There is no doubt that an in-sink garbage disposer is the cleanest, easiest, and quickest way to dispose of kitchen wastes. If space permits, you might also consider adding a trash compactor. Certainly, with the emphasis on recycling, you will need at least three bins to hold plastic, glass, and aluminum or

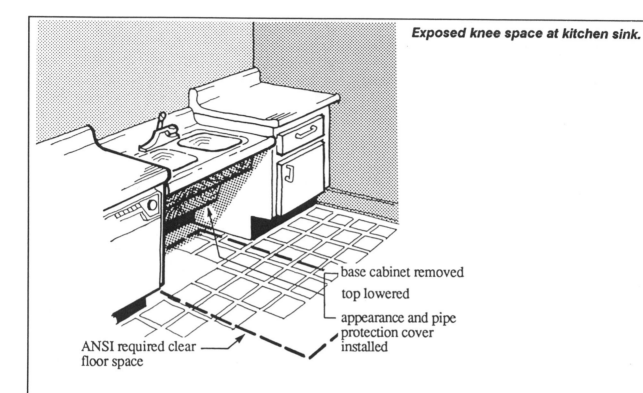

*Exposed knee space at kitchen sink.*

base cabinet removed

top lowered

appearance and pipe protection cover installed

ANSI required clear floor space

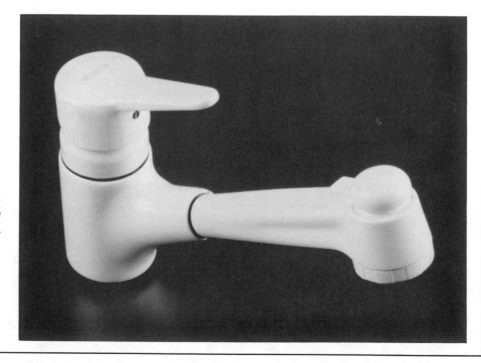

*Single-lever kitchen faucet has integrated protection against scalding and a ceramic disc cartridge for reliability. The faucet also has a flexible pull-out sprayer. Photo courtesy of Blanco.*

*A worker at the Conklin Center for the multi-handi-capped blind aids a student in operating cooktop controls. Photo courtesy of Whirlpool Corp.*

*A resident of the Conklin Center prepares lunch in a microwave oven equipped with Braille control overlays. Photo courtesy of Whirlpool Corp.*

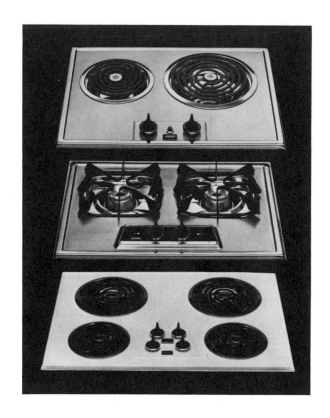

*Cooktops feature up-front controls and staggered burners for safe operation by the elderly or less able. Top and bottom units are electric; the center unit is gas. Electric cooktops are recommended for those whose sense of smell is impaired, as those persons would not detect gas leaks. Photo courtesy of Whirlpool Corp.*

*Cast iron cooking elements provide a choice of cooking heat: there are one 2600-watt, one 2000-watt, and two 1500-watt units. Up-front controls and black burners against the white glass cooktop provide a high degree of visual contrast to help prevent accidents.*

Small appliances, often called "countertop appliances," can clutter the countertop and may have potential for burns or other injuries. Don't let appliance cords hang: fold the excess cord up neatly and secure the folded section with a twist-tie or rubber band. Fold-up appliance shelves to hold mixers or other appliances can provide ease of access plus keep countertops clear and accident-free. Clocks, knife sharpeners, and coffee makers can be mounted under upper cabinets where they will be easily accessible but secured against accidents. If you like a TV in the kitchen, be sure to have remote control to avoid frequent tuning trips across the kitchen.

Some small appliances that can substitute for major appliances include:

- portable range — choose a tabletop two-burner model with front controls and dials that are easy to turn

- electric skillet — choose one with detachable control and a sturdy base

- compact (bar-type) refrigerator

- toaster oven

- other countertop range

## LAUNDRY

The barrier-free house will have the laundry on the main floor or in the bathroom, not stuck away in a basement. Compact laundry equipment such as the stacked washer/dryer shown can be fitted into a closet or a corner of the bath or kitchen. Such companion items as pull-out or fold-down ironing boards keep iron and board concealed but readily accessible. A pull-out shelf or drawer to hold laundry detergent and supplies will complete the laundry needs. If remodeling an existing house to be barrier-free, the water supply and drain pipes plus electric wiring must be rerouted to the closet or other laundry location.

## ELECTRICAL OUTLETS

Today's electrical codes require that all outlets near plumbing or water use have ground fault circuit interrupters (GFCI's). There are fuses or circuit breakers at your electrical service entrance panel, and these fuses will blow (or circuit breakers snap) to protect your house from electrical fires in the event of faulty appliances or any short in the electrical system. These devices will not protect a person from dangerous or even fatal electrical shock. GFCI's, on the other hand, sense if any electrical current goes to ground at a particular outlet or point of usage. In an electrical circuit that is functioning properly there are two wires: one is called neutral (white in color), and the other is hot (black). If current does not go to ground, there is as much current returning to the service panel via the neutral (white) wire as is being sent to the outlet via the hot (black) wire. If the circuit fails there is shock potential at the outlet or appliance. Electrical current may travel to ground via the human body, causing injury or death. But the GFCI measures current flow on both wires and senses any drop in current along the neutral wire. A drop of four milliamps on the neutral wire will cause the circuit interrupter (GFCI) to stop the current before serious shock can result.

If your house is older it may not have GFCI protection in kitchen, bath, or laundry. You can buy GFCI outlets at electrical supply stores, and they are quite easy to install. Follow the directions included with the GFCI. They can be installed so they protect only one outlet, or they can also protect all outlets downstream from the box where the device is installed. If you don't feel comfortable about doing this work, call an electrician.

*Appliances in the independent living apartment at the Conklin Center for the multi-handicapped blind have raised dots at temperature settings and Braille overlays on appliance controls. Photo courtesy of Whirlpool Corp.*

*Wooden shelf pulls out below microwave, providing a handy spot for setting hot dishes. Photo courtesy of Whirlpool Corp.*

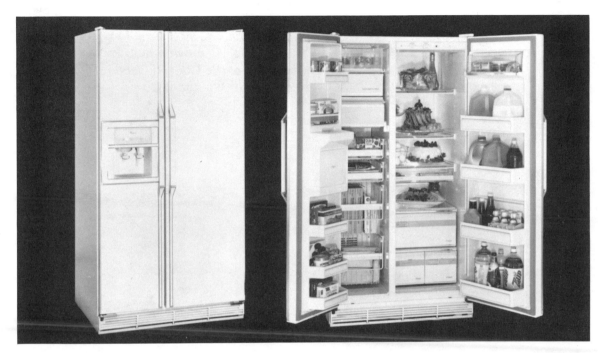

*Side-by-side construction and exterior ice/water dispensers make this refrigerator accessible. Inside, pull-out shelves, bins, and baskets plus gallon-size door bins provide extra accessibility. Photo courtesy of Whirlpool Corp.*

*This side-by-side refrigerator and freezer offer low-level access to a person in a wheelchair. The counter-maker compartment provides easy access to frequently used items. The unit has sealed fruit and vegetable pans, a sealed snack pan, and sealed storage dishes. Photo courtesy of Hotpoint.*

*This washer and dryer have large graphics on the controls, lid instructions, and use and care guide. All provide help for the visually impaired at the Conklin Center. Photo courtesy of Whirlpool Corp.*

*This washer/dryer is only 27 inches wide and occupies half the space of a conventional laundry pair. The laundry can be tucked into a closet, kitchen, or bathroom to keep it accessible for the less able. Photo courtesy of Sears.*

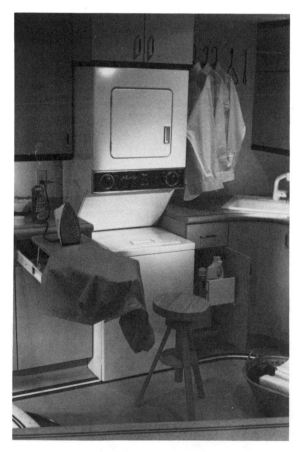

*Stacking washer/dryer tucks into a corner of the kitchen. The slide-out ironing board, clothes bin, and presoak sink make the laundry area extra useful. Photo courtesy of Whirlpool Corp.*

### Hire an Electrician

If you are making an older house barrier-free, it may be advisable to hire a professional electrician to bring your electrical system up to code. This means not only installing ground fault protection in the areas mentioned but also changing outlet or switch locations to a more reachable height, adding extra outlets for more convenience, installing lighting under upper cabinets or over sinks or other work areas, upgrading light levels for those with reduced light perception, installing the circuit box or panel on the first floor of the house (rather than the garage or outside), and installing oversized switch plates, time-activated or motion-detecting outdoor lighting, or installing low-voltage path or feature lighting along walks, drive, or gardens.

While the electrician is at work, have him hook up any convenience items that your house lacks, such as an in-sink garbage disposer, trash compactor, intercom speakers, and the like. Remember, too, that points such as the height of electrical outlets from the floor are decided more from custom than from need. You may wish to have wall outlets moved so they are higher off the floor than the familiar 12" to 16" height: outlets set at 24" or more above the floor are handier for those who have difficulty in bending or stooping.

Be sure also that you can control kitchen lighting from any doorway to the kitchen. Have the electrician install two-way or three-way switches, depending on the number of entry doors, so you can turn lights on and off from any entry point.

## ORGANIZERS

For those with limited mobility, lower cabinets with all drawers or pull-out trays can be handier than cabinets with doors and shelves. If the kitchen cabinets are stock items, with doors and shelves, and will be retained, remove the shelves and install vinyl or epoxy-coated wire baskets that swivel or pull out. Check your kitchen remodeling center carefully and choose just the pull-out organizers that you need to fit your particular lifestyle. Options include wire vegetable bins; pull-out shelves with racks to hold dishes, pots, or canned goods; door-hanging shelves for storing food or cleaning supplies; and multiple bins for recycling trash. Mount a trash receptacle inside the door of a low cabinet to save floor space. Pull-up brackets are available to hold small appliances, and the brackets fold away under countertops to avoid clutter on the countertop. Other storage options include roll-out racks and bins, shelf trays, lazy susans, and baskets.

## FLOORING

It should go without saying that the barrier-free house should have non-slip, no-trip floors. Having once broken a leg after slipping on a freshly waxed floor, I am rather critical of some of the flooring materials that are available today. Kitchen carpet is tightly woven, offers some sound control as well as firm footing, and is inexpensive and attractive. A good grade of vinyl inlay floor covering can be perfectly safe, if properly maintained and cleaned.

Don't hesitate to ask your floor covering dealer for a look at vinyl coverings that are generally reserved for use in institutions such as hospitals. These floor coverings are not only more slip-resistant, but are superior in construction to stand up to commercial traffic.

Wood flooring has staged a resurgence in popularity and is perfectly safe and comfortable underfoot if kept clean and maintained. If you choose wood flooring, be sure to follow the manufacturer's instructions for maintenance and cleaning.

*Pull-out wastebasket holds 30 quarts of trash. Photo courtesy of Merillat Industries.*

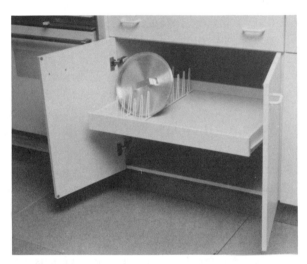

*Pot lid rack fits into a base pull-out tray and holds up to nine pot lids or baking pans. Photo courtesy of Merillat Industries.*

*Spice rack, shown here mounted on an upper door, could be mounted on a base cabinet door for easy wheelchair access. Photo courtesy of Merillat Industries.*

*Base cabinets with drawers may be preferable to doors for family members who cannot easily bend or kneel to retrieve needed cooking items. Photo courtesy of Merillat Industries.*

*Use swivel-out wire shelves in corner cabinets to replace a lazy susan. Shelves such as these eliminate awkward reaching to retrieve items. Photo courtesy of Clairson International.*

*Fitted into larger spaces, pull-out baskets improve both visibility and accessibility of stored items. Photo courtesy of Clairson International.*

*Handy hanging shelves can be attached to the inside of doors for easy access. If you plan to load up door shelves with weight, consider adding extra hinges or piano hinges to ensure enough support. Photo courtesy of Clairson International.*

*Double slide-out baskets fit into narrow cabinet space and provide access without stooping. Photo courtesy of Clairson International.*

*Vinyl-coated wire baskets may glide, lift, or swivel out and can be purchased installed or as do-it-yourself kits. Photo courtesy of Clairson International.*

*Glide-out access can be had by removing cabinet shelves and installing coated wire baskets. Use the baskets or pull-out shelves in kitchen or bathroom cabinets. Photo courtesy of Clairson International.*

## DECORATING

Light colors — whites, creams, light beiges — are generally more cheerful in the kitchen, and have a higher level of light reflectivity, both characteristics being desirable for those who spend much time at home or shut in. Because the less able often don't have the mobility to do their own heavy cleaning, use paints or wall coverings that are scrubbable. Paints are more easily cleaned if they are of high sheen, so choose paints that are semi-gloss or high gloss for the easiest maintenance. Vinyl wall coverings are usually either washable (meaning they can be sponge cleaned) or scrubbable, which means you can be very vigorous in the cleaning attack. Do not underestimate the value of a good cleanable surface: I have seen wall covering that was twenty-five years old that was still presentable and clean, only slightly worn from repeated hard scrubbings.

## CHECKLIST
# THE KITCHEN

❑ Countertops are most useful if their height is varied. For example, a low counter by the sink, for preparing salads or vegetables, is mandatory for a person in a wheelchair but useful for any cook.

❑ Leave leg room under countertops, especially at the sink. This can be done by removing the face from sink cabinets or by eliminating sink cabinets altogether.

❑ Pull-out trays permit better access than standard shelving and doors/drawers on cabinets.

❑ Do not have countertops and floors of matching colors. There should be a clean color break between the two surfaces, so visually impaired people can distinguish where the counter edge ends.

❑ Install baskets and swing-out organizers, rather than shelving, in base cabinets. These organizers increase the storage capacity through better organization, while aiding access to needed food items or utensils.

❑ Install wall-mounted ovens and microwaves. This allows for installation at the best height for wheelchair access.

❑ Use all electric cooking appliances. Persons with poor sense of smell may not detect gas leaks.

❑ Buy a cooktop with staggered burners, so you will not have to reach over a hot front burner to get to a back burner.

❑ Cooktops should have controls at the front or side of the unit, for easy accessibility by a seated person.

❑ Hot water dispensers at the sink will reduce the danger of burn injuries, simplify snack and beverage preparation.

❑ Keep countertop appliances such as toasters or toaster ovens in appliance garages, to prevent damage to the appliances or burn injuries to the cook. Do not let appliance cords hang loose; use a rubber band or twist-tie to secure excess cord.

❑ Equip all kitchen electrical outlets with ground fault circuit interrupters (GFCI's).

❑ If there is no room for a bathroom laundry, consider putting the laundry in the kitchen. An unused pantry can be plumbed to hold stackable laundry appliances.

❑ Select a floor covering that is both slip-resistant and easily maintained. Consider the institutional vinyls and ceramic tiles before making a final choice.

❑ Be sure there is adequate task lighting to prevent accidents and burns in the kitchen. High level lighting is a must at the sink and cutting board, and around cooking appliances.

❑ Keep a fire extinguisher in the kitchen.

# 5
# Closets and Storage

If you have trouble finding clothes or stored items in your closet, it may be time to de-junk and get organized. The very first step in making closets accessible is to sell, give, or throw away unused items. Never love anything that can't love you back: be absolutely ruthless in discarding junk.

## CLOSETS

When you have reduced your clothing and storage bulk to an absolute minimum, clean out your closets. Remove the top shelf and hanging pole, and install (or have installed) the neat closet organizers that are available today. The double clothes pole, with one pole just over three feet from the floor, is just what is needed in a barrier-free house. Low shelves and clothes poles that are easily reached while seated are ideal for those confined to a wheelchair.

Bi-fold, pocket, or sliding doors take up less room and are less in the way than hinged doors. In addition to installing closet organizers, you may want to exchange the doors for one of these other types. If doors are not a necessity, you might want to use lightweight draw draperies on a ceiling track instead.

If you have a medium-sized closet, consider installing the Closet Carousel, a motor-driven affair that brings your clothes to you at the push of a button. The carousels are available in any of ten different sizes, with the minimum space requirement being 4'6" x 6'. There are available attachments that fit onto the carousel and permit you to customize the storage space to your own particular needs.

Almost as handy as the carousel is the walk-in closet. Shelves and hanging rods can be set at varying heights to accommodate any variety of situations. With multi-level storage, several people can share the space, with space divided according to individual height limitations and general needs.

If you have a closet that is deep, at least 3½ feet from front to back, you may regret the wasted space. Most modern closets are built so they accept suits or skirts on hangers, so closets are built to single-hanger depth or 24 inches. Deeper closets can be made more useful by installing a clothes rod so it hangs 12 inches on center from the back wall. If the closet has a single rod, hang it no higher than 48 inches from the floor, with a shelf 3 inches above the rod. (In a child's room, hang the rod 30 to 36 inches above the floor.) You may even install a double pole setup, with one pole set about 36 inches above the floor, and a second pole set about 78 inches above the floor. Then install a StorMate unit (see photo) in front of the hanging poles. The StorMate units are basically chests

*The Closet Carousel● brings your clothes to you at the push of a button. It comes in ten sizes and will fit in a space as small as 4'6 x 6'. Photo courtesy of White Home Products.*

*Basket and/or shoe rack attachments can be added to the Closet Carousel● to customize it. Photo courtesy of White Home Products.*

*Walk-in storage closet is ideal for wheelchair access. Adjustable steel shelving lets you set shelf height for the convenience of any family member. Photo courtesy of White Home Products.*

*Fully-shelved closet with pull-out carts on casters permits wheelchair to enter and keeps items used by the less able reachable on low shelves. Photo courtesy of White Home Products.*

*If you have a deep closet with wasted space, StorMate® built-ins can maximize storage. They are mounted on tracks so they can be moved aside for access to rear storage. Photo courtesy of White Home Products.*

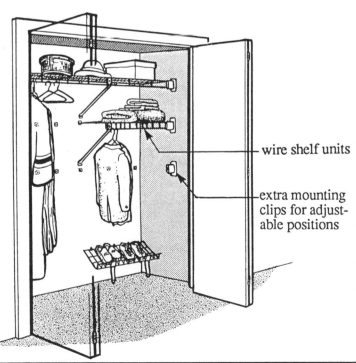

wire shelf units

extra mounting clips for adjustable positions

*Accessible storage in closets using vinyl-coated wire shelving.*

that fit on a floor track and can be pushed from side to side for access to storage at the back of the closet. The chests can hold clothes in drawers or in shelves, and the units can virtually double the storage capacity of the closet.

Surfaces in a closet should be smooth but not slippery. Items stored on shelves should slide off easily but not so fast that they create a hazard.

Don't overlook lights for dark closets. If you have your older wiring updated, have the electrician install closet lights where there are none, or install switches to replace pull-chain fixtures. Also available are battery-powered lights for use where rewiring would be difficult. For the utmost in closet lighting convenience, install door switches that turn lights on and off when the door is opened and shut.

The closet doorway should not have a sill or threshold. If the adjoining room is carpeted, run the carpet into the closet as well.

## STORAGE

Storage devices are available that can be assembled in almost any configuration. Adjustable shelf brackets, combined with steel or wire shelving, can be assembled so that shelves or a desk can be at any height, to make a home office. Coated wire baskets make excellent storage devices.

You can find under-bed storage modules that are fitted with casters and can be rolled under the bed when needed, or place a bank of dressers against a wall to provide low level storage and easy access.

**CHECKLIST**

# CLOSETS AND STORAGE

❑ Install bifold or sliding doors on closets. Louvered closet doors are best in damp climates.

❑ If space permits, install a carousel in the closet to permit you to review your wardrobe at the flick of a switch.

❑ Walk-in closets should be roomy enough for wheelchair entry.

❑ Provide good lighting in closets. Consider battery-powered lighting if the closet is not wired for lighting.

❑ Install closet poles at a height accessible to wheelchair occupants.

❑ Use wire baskets, shelves, and trays rather than wood or steel shelving to hold clothes; they provide ventilation and help you locate clothing at a glance.

❑ If you have deep closets with wasted space, install clothes poles at the back of the closet and install cabinets on tracks at the front of the closet.

❑ Equip each closet with a reach extender that has a crab-claw hook to help you reach and retrieve clothes from any level.

❑ Look for closet organizers with adjustable shelves, so you can configure storage to meet your needs.

❑ Paint closet interiors white or a very light color to increase visibility of the contents.

❑ Check out under-bed storage drawers. These drawer units have casters that permit them to roll under the bed; they are space-saving and easily accessible.

❑ Buy wicker or cedar chests to replace coffee and end tables. These items look good and offer easily accessible storage.

❑ To stretch closet space in bedrooms, assemble seasonal wardrobes and build off-season storage shelves or closets in the basement or attic.

❑ Clean clothes before storing them. Avoid clutter by giving away clothes you seldom wear.

# 6
# Around the House

In prior chapters we have considered specific points where barrier-free efforts are most critical. The critical areas are those that have the highest levels of traffic and activity: exterior walks, steps, and entry; halls and stairways; bathrooms; kitchen; and closets. Ideally, the entire house should be barrier-free, simply because removing barriers is of benefit to everyone who will live in the house.

## DOORS

Double entry doors are a plus for those with limited mobility, but a person in a wheelchair can negotiate any 36-inch wide door. This is not only true at entry doors: wider doors are better at all rooms. Bathrooms, bedrooms, and closets can have doors that are 32 inches wide, providing there is a wide (4-foot) hall that permits a turn to be made before entering the narrower door. If you have standard 3-foot wide halls, you can either make the hall wider, or install 36-inch doors to permit turning and entry for wheelchairs.

As noted elsewhere, pocket, sliding, or bi-fold doors are preferable to the ordinary hinged version, a door that swings into the room and thus takes up space. Some experts suggest hinging bathroom doors to swing out, into the hall, rather than swinging into limited bathroom space.

## Remove Unneeded Doors

One way to gain extra space, simplify passage between rooms, and make small rooms look larger is to remove any unneeded doors. For example, postwar tract houses were often built with a center bedroom that had two doors: one opening into the kitchen, the other into the center hall. This setup permitted young families to use the space either as a third bedroom or nursery or as an eating area accessible from the kitchen. In one such house I decided to use that space as a small dining room, which meant that the two doors were unnecessary for privacy. I removed both doors, used latex wood filler to fill in the hinge mortises in the door jamb, and painted the door jamb and trim. The result is two wood-trimmed openings, with no doors. With the doors removed the room seems larger, and the removed doors were just an unneeded nuisance.

Survey your own home and decide whether doors into dens, dining space, or family rooms are needed. I have a door on a bedroom-turned-TV den. The door interferes with furniture placement when open, because it opens back against a wall. Yet the door has never been closed in the six years I have lived in the house. Often, doors decrease the actual door width by the thickness of the door and hinge extension, so removing the door may mean the difference between being accessible or impossible for entry by a person in a wheelchair.

For resale, I stored my unused doors in a basement storeroom, in the event that a future buyer prefers to use the space as a bedroom and wishes to replace the doors.

### Entry Doors

Particularly in colder climates, entry doors may consist of two doors: the entry door plus a combination or "storm" door. The combination door serves as both a screen door and a secondary barrier to cold weather. But combination doors often have openers on them, openers that may interfere with entry when they are mounted low or restrict the door so it cannot be fully opened. If the combination door is a problem you can replace the primary door with one that is made of either fiberglass or metal and has a foam insulation core. The insulated doors often are more energy efficient than the old two-door setup, while eliminating the need for the combination door. Shop for metal doors by companies such as Pease or for fiberglass doors by Therma-Tru Corp.

# WINDOWS

Double-hung windows are the most common type seen in older houses. They are the windows that can be opened from the top down or from the bottom up by moving either top or bottom sash in its tracks. The older versions of these windows may rattle and leak cold air inside, or they may stick and be almost impossible to operate for those with reduced strength or mobility. New double-hung windows are properly weather-stripped and may have adjustment screws in the tracks that can adjust the tension on the window sash, making them easier to open. Proper cleaning and lubrication of the window hardware will also make them easier to operate.

But if you are planning to build or remodel, consider using casement windows that have either cranks or pull levers that permit you to open the window while seated. Make sure window sills are not more than 36 inches from the floor so a person seated in a wheelchair can see out.

Horizontal sliding windows usually have their handles mounted halfway up the window. If you have this type, consider mounting another D-shaped handle at the bottom of the window for easier maneuvering.

Roof or skylight windows are another popular option that can increase light levels. They can be opened for air circulation and ventilation. Some roof windows can be equipped with power openers and remote control devices. Check out such brands as Velux, Anderson, and Pella.

### Window Coverings

For window coverings, the person with limited mobility does not want blinds, topped with sheers, topped with draperies. The best choices for window coverings are roll-up shades with long cords (make sure the cords are properly secured if small children are present), tailored tieback curtains, lightweight draw draperies with good hardware and an easy to reach cord, and louvered blinds.

Mini-blinds can reduce glare from direct sunlight while still offering good visibility to the outside. The blinds can also be closed to ensure the privacy and security demanded by seniors and others.

# HARDWARE AND LOCKS

We have mentioned that knob pulls on kitchen cabinet doors and drawers can be a barrier to those who have limited grip. Replace all knob pulls on cabinetry such as kitchen and bathroom cabinets with "D" (sometimes called "C") shaped pulls. These pulls are easier to operate than small pull knobs.

Pull handle hardware is also available for replacement on furniture such as wardrobe chests. You can also inspect the track hardware on drawers, and clean and lubricate the tracks and rollers as needed. For drawers without metal tracks, where wood drawers slide on wood guides, lubricate the wood contact surfaces with carpenter's wax (beeswax) or a candle stub. Periodic maintenance can reduce sticking drawers and doors that bind.

## Locks

Door locks can be a frustrating barrier to those with poor coordination, reduced gripping strength, or failing eyesight. Consider using push-button, numbered code door locks at entries. Round door knobs can also be difficult to turn for those with arthritic hands. Perhaps most difficult to handle for the aged are the locks with thumb-levers, which can require great hand strength to operate, especially so as the locks age.

Lever-type door handles are the easiest to use. Choose a lock with lever handles long enough to be operated with a push of the elbow or the edge of the hand.

Entry door locks are not the only lock barriers we meet. All round knobs, even on interior privacy or passage (room) doors can offer obstacles. Replace all interior door knobs with lever-type locks, or check out add-on levers that can be mounted over existing round door knobs. These lever add-ons cost under $15 each and are excellent, low-cost alternatives to lock replacement. The lever add-ons are easy to install and require no carpentry skills.

## FLOOR COVERING

Almost any of the popular flooring options can be used in barrier-free houses, if you select the product with care. Vinyl floor covering is available for institutional use and is designed to be durable, at-tractive, and non-slip. Ceramic tiles with non-slip finishes are also a viable option for entry, kitchen, or bath flooring, as are the various hardwood flooring options. The prime consideration in floor safety is keeping the flooring clean and properly maintained. We have discussed this to some extent in other chapters.

Two things we could add, however. The first is *never* to use throw or scatter rugs on floors where people of limited mobility must walk. Throw rugs represent hazards both from tripping and from slipping, if the rug slips from underfoot when placed on a slippery surface.

The second factor to keep in mind is that any changes in floor level, such as a transition between a vinyl floor and one that has thick carpeting can be hazardous. While this small transition may be unnoticed by those of us who are fully ambulatory, they may provide a tripping barrier for those with a hesitant or shuffling gait. Nailing a 3/8-inch layer of plywood over the existing kitchen or bath floor can bring the vinyl floor more even with the carpeted living or dining room floor. When you install new non-slip floor covering, consider laying lauan plywood over the old floor covering, rather than trying to remove it.

## LIGHTING

We have discussed outdoor or entrance lighting in the first chapter and the need for focused work lighting in the kitchen. Good lighting is needed on the countertop in areas where food is prepared and over stoves or cooktops where lack of clear vision could result in a painful burn or scalding from spilled food. In addition, night lights in halls or in bedrooms of those who are often up at night can eliminate falls caused by darkness and poor visibility.

Remove all low furniture such as footstools, coffee tables, or magazine racks from the walking path, or remove them altogether. These low items are hard to see in the dark and can represent a real tripping hazard to the unsteady. I prefer to install dimming switches on all my lights and use them at low level for night lights in halls or bathrooms. Buy the dimming switches that have built-in lights in the switch toggles, so you can easily find them in the dark without fumbling.

Buy lamps that operate at a touch. Any lamp that has a metal base can be adapted to touch control by adding an adapter. There are also devices that operate lights by voice command. Telephones, too, are available with a light that flashes with each ring, making the device easy to find in the dark. Other lighting options include those with motion-sensors. These can be used inside as a convenience item or on the exterior for both convenience and as a home security measure.

### Electrical Outlets

Modern electrical codes insist on having electrical outlets spaced no more than 12 feet apart. The purpose of this is to eliminate the need for extension cords for lamps and household appliances. People tend to abuse extension cords, pulling them out by the wire rather than pulling on the plug or leaving them on the floor where they become worn and dangerous. Have house wiring updated to ensure you have plenty of outlets and need no extension cords. This step is important for preventing electrical shocks as well as eliminating a primary fire (and/or tripping) hazard. While you're having the wiring updated, don't neglect to install ground fault circuit interrupters (GFCI's) not only in the bathroom, laundry, and kitchen but also in the garage, in the workshop, and on exterior electrical outlets used to run lawn tools and such.

Strip outlets are available for under-cabinet use, where you need outlets for small kitchen appliances. Add the extra outlets when you wire in new lighting for under-counter or over-sink lights.

## FAUCETS

We've talked about anti-scald valves for burn prevention while in the tub or shower. There are also anti-scald controls in bath and kitchen faucets. The best insurance against burns is to turn the water heater thermostat down so the water is not hot enough to injure you. Drop the thermostat down to 120 degrees. If hot water must be mixed with cold to be tolerated on skin, or if steam comes out of faucets when you turn them on, your water temperature is at dangerous levels and could badly burn any person who might have difficulty moving quickly out of harm's way.

### Faucet Controls

All faucets in the house should have U-shaped or single lever controls. Ordinary faucet handles of glass or chrome may be slippery and hard to operate for those with diminished gripping power. Lever faucets let you control both water volume and temperature levels with one hand. If necessary, the lever handle can be operated by a push of the elbow or the fist.

Some faucets can be operated by infrared sensors, of the type often found in public places such as restaurant or athletic club restrooms. The automatic faucets sometimes offer either manual or sensor controls, depending on the needs of the operator. When you place your hands by the sensors at the base of the faucet, the faucet flows. These faucets have preset water flow and temperature control. One such model is called the Cue-Tel. It is available from:

Columbia Electronic Research Group, Ltd.
50 Doughty Blvd.
Lawrence, NY 11559

Other kitchen faucets have pull-out extensions that let you fill deep kettles or pails. These options can be useful for filling scrub or cleaning pails without moving to the laundry or utility area.

## APPLIANCES

We've talked about the features that make major appliances more accessible for all. Hand-held or countertop appliances are available with wall mounts to keep them always plugged in, always at hand. Items such as mixers and toasters can be stored in countertop appliance "garages" that are built into the cabinetry.

Appliances such as toaster ovens and clothes irons generate heat, and thus can be a fire hazard. Such appliances are available today with automatic shutoff switches, which are an aid to the forgetful or distracted. Appliances with this automatic shut-off feature cost little more than standard models but can be a source of comfort if you are one who worries whether you shut off the iron when you leave home.

## FIRE SAFETY

Fire safety begins with smoke or fire alarms placed strategically throughout the house. The most common points for fire to begin are in furnace/utility rooms, in kitchens, and in attached garages. For smokers, the fire hazards can extend to the bedroom and family rooms where people congregate and smoke.

Install smoke detectors on all floors of the house. Place alarms near furnace or heating equipment, at the top of any stairs, in attached or tuck-under garages, and in the kitchen. Because most fires occur at night when people are sleeping — between 10 p.m. and 6 a.m. — fire or smoke alarms should also be located in hallways that serve bedrooms, just outside of bedroom doors. Some smoke detectors include a built-in escape light that comes on when the alarm is triggered.

Fire or smoke alarms can be wired into the electrical service of your house — called "hard wired" — or can be battery operated. If you choose the hard-wired type, purchase one with a built-in battery backup in case of power failure. If you choose battery-operated alarms, be aware of the need to test the alarm frequently (at least once a month) to be sure the battery is still charged. The National Fire Protection Association recommends that you change the batteries in your smoke detectors each year at the daylight-to-standard time change. There have been many fire reports that tell of faulty or non-operating alarms, either disconnected or having dead batteries. On battery-operated alarms there is a test button that can be pushed to see if the alarm activates. Testing the batteries should be a part of routine home maintenance. Smoke detectors are available with strobe lights that flash to alert the hearing-impaired person.

Special electrical outlets are available that can be wired directly to a fire-alarm system. In the bedroom, such a system could trigger a fan or bed-vibrating mechanism plugged into the special outlet to alert the sleeping resident in case of fire. This could be helpful for anyone.

One product on the market could be especially useful for the disabled user. The Eveready Battery Co. markets the Eversafe Child Locator. Designed to be used in a child's room, it is equally useful for any person who might need extra help escaping a fire. The device combines a smoke detector, which is mounted on the ceiling of the bedroom, with a flashing red locater light, which attaches to the bedroom window with suction cups. When the smoke detector goes off, it triggers the flashing light, alerting rescue personnel. This product is available from:

Eveready Battery Co. Inc.
39 Old Ridebury Road
Danbury, CT 06817-0001
(203) 794-2000

Be sure that all upholstery and bedding in the house is fire retardant. Install fire extinguishers on all levels of the house and check to be sure they are charged. It is estimated that one-third of house fires occur in the kitchen, so install a fire extinguisher at a level that can be reached by any adult family member.

Flame retardant chemicals are available in pump-type containers. Flame retardants can be used on furniture, upholstery, drapes, or mattresses. There are also flame retardants that can be used on live Christmas trees.

## HOME SECURITY

Security is a concern for us everyone and is a special concern for the elderly. You can find home security experts in the Yellow Pages, listed under "Security Control Equipment & Systems." Nationally recognized companies that sell and install security equipment for the home include: Brink's Home Security Systems, Bell Security Systems, Honeywell Protection Services, and Mitsubishi Electronic.

Brink's, the nationally known security company, has a home security system that sells for around $200. The basic system includes three perimeter sensors, an interior motion detector, an automatic warning siren, a master control unit, a backup power supply, and warning signs to deter prowlers. There is a monthly monitoring fee charged to monitor the system.

### Security Systems

Security systems can be wired into your house or operate wireless. Check with local police for advice on crime statistics in your area. Often, lighting that lights when it detects motion or electric eye lights that provide dusk-to-dawn lighting will deter amateur burglars. Deadbolt locks provide better security than ordinary passage locks, because the bolts extend through the jamb and into the jack studs that frame the door. Garage door openers let you enter your home without leaving your ve-

hicle, provide entry lighting, and are difficult to force entry.

In most communities house burglaries are committed by young amateurs who seek easy targets, and if you take even basic precautionary measures these burglars will seek easier targets.

Check the following references for more information on home security:

*The Complete Guide to Home Security: How to Protect Your Home and Family from Harm*, by David Alan Wacker (1990, Betterway Publications, Inc.)

*The Complete Watchdog's Guide to Installing Your Own Home Burglar Alarm*, by David Petraglia (1984, Prentice-Hall, Inc.)

*Security: Everything You Need to Know About Household Alarm Systems*, by Tom Lewin (1982, Park Lane Enterprises)

*Security Systems: Considerations, Layout, and Performance*, by William J. Cook, Jr., (1982, Howard W. Sams & Co.)

## CLEANING

To ease cleaning chores, consider installing a built-in vacuum cleaner. While canister or upright vacuum cleaners must be stored away and moved about the house for cleaning, the central or built-in vacuum cleaner lets you locate all heavy or bulky components in an attached garage or other remote area. This isolates the noise from the living area, and lets you carry only the hose and nozzle attachment through the house. Wall outlets installed in every major room let you connect the vacuum hose and appropriate attachment and move only the hose around the room to clean. This moving of reduced weight, without the motor and housing, can make vacuuming much easier for those with reduced strength in arms or hands.

Keep in mind that most of the dirt the vacuum picks up was carried into the house on your shoes. If door mats at the entries are a barrier to any family member, install a foot scraper at the entrances. Choose one of those foot scrapers that has stiff bristle brushes at the bottom and both sides to clean the shoes thoroughly. You can greatly reduce cleaning chores by cleaning debris from shoes before it is tracked across the floors.

You can also reduce cleaning chores by choosing interior finishes with cleaning and maintenance in mind. Probably the lowest maintenance flooring is carpeting, which needs only periodic vacuuming. But if carpet is not kept clean, it can collect dust and molds which can be a real problem for those who have any allergies or respiratory problems.

Keeping air clean can reduce cleaning chores, too. Forced air furnaces can become dust machines if filters are not changed frequently. If you check above the air registers in dirty houses you can see black dirt streaks up the wall, carried there by dust-laden air. Change furnace filters at least every thirty days during heating season or monthly, year round, if your furnace also incorporates central air conditioning.

# FURNITURE

The size of the room should determine where furniture will be located. If the room is small, leave the center of the room open for easy traffic flow and place the furniture around the edges. If the room is large, put the furniture in a center "island" with 4- to 5-foot wide areas for traffic flow around the perimeter of the room. You may want to put tables and small furniture on casters so they will be easy to move.

## Shelves

Book shelves in the barrier-free home should be easily accessible. The lowest shelves should be mounted at least 10 inches above floor level, and the highest should be mounted no more than 48 inches above the floor. The depth should be about 16 inches, although narrower shelves may be especially useful for books and similar items.

## Sofas and Chairs

The best height for the seats of sofas and chairs is about 18 inches from the floor, especially for the elderly and those who use crutches, canes, or braces. The seats should be firm rather than soft, so the person can rise easily.

To adjust the height of a chair to the user's comfort, cut down the legs to lower the chair or firmly attach the legs to blocks or a platform to raise it. Don't add a thick cushion to the seat to raise the height; this will put the chair's arms at an uncomfortable height.

Recliner chairs are a good choice as they are generally firm, heavy, and stable. You might want to look into upholstered chairs generally used as office furniture, as they are often heavier and higher than standard home furnishings. Check the Yellow Pages under "Office Furniture."

## Desks

Drop-front or wide kneehole desks are generally best for the wheelchair occupant. The top surface of the desk should be about 32 inches from the floor, with a clearance of 29½ inches from the surface of the desk to the floor (this will permit the wheelchair's arm rests to slide under the desk's surface). Wheelchair occupants and most others will need a minimum of 24 inches of front to back depth for their feet and legs.

Desks and tables with a U-shaped front cutout may be the most comfortable for children and adults. The wrap-around sides of the desk provide extra support for the arms and shoulders, and books and papers are easier to reach. You can make a wrap-around surface by topping a steady table with a sheet of plywood with the U shape cut out.

## Beds

The top surface of a bed's mattress should be even with the height of the wheelchair seat for a wheelchair user. The bed can be raised on blocks (be sure the bed is securely attached to the blocks) or a platform to bring the mattress up to the proper height. The mattress should, of course, be firm.

For transfer from a wheelchair, about 3½ feet minimum clearance is needed between the side of the bed and the wall or the side of the bed and other furniture. A firm, steady headboard is often a boon to the physically limited. Grab bars can be added to the headboard if necessary.

## Control Center and Intercom

A control center in the bedroom or main living area is often a boon to the physically handicapped and elderly. It can include a console for controlling a variety of electrical items including lamps, air conditioner, TV, stereo, etc. Some control centers can even allow access to the front door and can be combined with an intercom system for maximum security. See the Appendix for manufacturers of such systems.

## CHECKLIST
# AROUND THE HOUSE

❑ Always consider easy access when installing doors. Wide doors permit personal entry; bi-fold or sliding doors keep the door from getting in the way. The backside of closet doors can hold hanging bags or shelving to increase storage capacity.

❑ Avoid many-layered window coverings and draperies. Roll-up shades and mini-blinds are easy to operate.

❑ Choose D-shaped hardware pulls rather than round knobs or fold-away pulls that may be hard to grip.

❑ Choose lever-type door handles rather than round door knobs. The levers are easier to operate when hand grip is impaired.

❑ Install smoke detectors in all levels of your house. Have alarms outside bedrooms (in the hall), in laundry and furnace rooms, in the kitchen, and in an attached garage. Test each alarm at least once a month.

❑ Install electrical outlets at convenient heights to avoid having to stoop or bend to reach them. Electrical outlets are placed low to the floor by custom, not as a code requirement.

❑ Select products that arc casy to clean and maintain — non-stain carpets, upholstery fabric with Scotchgard® protection, no-wax flooring.

❑ Keep stairs and steps clean and well-lit. Don't store cleaning products or cleaning equipment on basement stairs where they become a tripping hazard.

❑ Install dimmer swithces on all lights. Dimmer switches save electricity, extend bulb life, and permit the light intensity to be adjusted. Buy switches with lighted toggles you can find in the dark, and turn the lights low for use as nighttime convenience lights.

❑ Consider ease of maintenance when buying any home products.

❑ Check *Consumer Reports* for frequency of repair listings on appliances, cars, etc. Buy with repair costs in mind.

❑ Read and heed owner's manuals for any tool or appliance you buy. Follow periodic maintenance instructions to prolong the item's life and reduce repair costs.

❑ Clean and lubricate hinges, locks, drawer tracks, windows, and appliance motors to keep them operating smoothly.

❑ Remove any doors that are not needed for privacy. Store the doors in a basement or storeroom so they're available to a future owner.

# 7
# Indoor Air Quality

When I was a high school student, my friend Tom returned to school each fall wearing turquoise buckles and Indian necklaces. Tom spent each summer on an Indian reservation in the Southwest, because the desert air was kinder to his asthma. In those days I could only imagine the plight of those who had allergies and respiratory ailments such as hay fever. Sometime past my fiftieth birthday I joined their unhappy ranks, and I no longer have to consult the daily pollen count to know when there is a pollen alert. As the poet once wrote, my nose knows.

Respiratory ailments often develop in those who are aging. And air pollution in your home often exceeds the levels you encounter on your freeway. Years ago, while working as a magazine editor, I received a report about a pollution engineer in Los Angeles, California. The engineer was wearing an air pollution monitor while touring the Los Angeles freeway system. He forgot to turn the monitor off when he arrived home and was surprised to find that the air inside his home was ten times more polluted than the freeway air. And as we tighten up our houses to conserve energy, the indoor air becomes even more polluted. Experts at the U.S. Environmental Protection Agency (EPA) tell us that the air pollution level can be as much as twenty times worse in your house than outdoors, and the source of that air pollution is usu-

ally under the direct control of the occupants of the house.

When I was a painting contractor I spray-textured ceilings. Most often we had to patch small cracks or nicks in the ceilings before we re-sprayed them. When we patched with a true white patching material on a ceiling in a house where smokers lived, we had to prime and seal the ceiling with an oil-base sealer before we could spray. The true white patches on the smoked-up ceilings would highlight through the nicotine stains on the ceilings, so the ceilings would dry to a yellow color while the patched areas remained pure white. If you are a smoker and doubt the effect cigarette smoke has on indoor air and cleanliness, hold a piece of white paper up against your ceilings. You may be amazed to see how dirty those ceilings are. The moral should be obvious: There is more than one reason you should not smoke inside the house.

A Chicago-based architect who was active in environmental issues told me that gas cooktops were once required to have chimneys to carry away waste gases. In time the requirement was dropped from building codes because the appliance industry argued that gas cooking appliances were operated only intermittently and then for brief periods. The problem may be that winter, when the house is tightly closed against the weather, is the time when we often prepare large meals.

*This electronic air cleaner can remove airborne pollutant particles down to .01 micron in size — small enough to filter out smoke. Photo courtesy of White-Rodgers Div. of Emerson Electric Co.*

Who has not noticed the windows fogging over when the Thanksgiving turkey was baking? Also, today, we have greatly tightened up our houses to stop air infiltration and reduce energy consumption. The products of gas combustion are not the only villains, of course. Cooking also produces smoke and grease to foul the air and dirty the walls. Install a range exhaust hood in the kitchen and use it frequently while cooking to remove air pollutants.

Tobacco, cooking, and fireplace smoke can all pollute indoor air. Avoid frying foods, use the microwave to reduce cooking time and grease, don't smoke indoors, and don't light the fireplace on very cold nights, when the house is tightly closed against the weather.

Also, avoid using aerosol products indoors. Using paint strippers indoors can not only pollute the air and cause respiratory problems, the fumes can damage your furnace if they are drawn into the furnace during combustion.

When installing new products such as carpet or paneling, leave the material in the garage for a couple of day to get rid of the "new smell." Some chemicals used in manufacturing home materials — formaldehyde, for example — can contribute to indoor air pollution. When the materials have lost the new smell, they are probably no air pollution threat to most people. The question of dangers from air pollution often revolves around the health of the house's occupants.

If you have household pets be sure to keep them well-groomed. Dog and cat dander can cause allergic reactions in those with respiratory problems.

Keep carpets vacuumed: they can provide a haven for dust and dirt.

Change furnace filters often to keep them clean, or install a heavy-duty multi-layered filter.

## AIR CLEANERS

Electronic air cleaners can be installed in furnace air ducts or can be used free-standing. The filters are available in a variety of sizes to fit various size ducts without costly alteration. Some air cleaners, such as the White-Rogers model shown here, have optional charcoal filters to absorb odors from such sources as raw onions, burnt food, solvents, and cigarette smoke.

The air cleaner shown will remove 98 percent of larger pollution particles from the air. These pollutants include pollen, household dust, and lint. It will also remove 75 percent of small pollutants such as smoke from cooking or tobacco. These pollutants can be as small as .01 microns, much too small to be trapped in the ordinary furnace filter.

The electronic filter shown works in-line when it is installed in furnace return air ducts. The furnace blower motor pulls dust, smoke, and pollen into the air cleaner, where larger particles are trapped by a pre-filter screen. Smaller particles are charged with a positive charge then drawn into the cleaner's collecting section. In the collecting section a series of positive plates repels the charged particles, and they are driven onto negative plates that trap and hold them. The pollutants are held in the collecting section until the filter is cleaned. Most filters can be washed in a laundry tub or in the dishwasher.

The cost of air cleaners varies depending on type and size. Prices start at around $50 for non-powered filters. Ask a heating contractor to recommend a unit for your home. Remember, too, that electronic air cleaners, as well as other health aids, may be deductible items on your income tax if they are purchased on the advice of your physician.

# 8
# Building to Reduce Maintenance

The cost of building anything can be expressed in two simple parts: the cost of the material and the labor costs to install the material. I had not been long in the building business when it dawned on me that the cost of building labor is pretty much a constant — that is, it takes X number of hours to install a window, no matter what the cost or quality of the window. It follows, therefore, that if you build with lower quality or cheaper materials and components, the only thing you are saving is the difference in cost between the cheap product and the quality product.

Let me cite an example. How many faucets are there in your house, not counting the laundry — just in the kitchen and bath(s)? The total is probably four faucets, counting the tub faucet, if you have a bath and a half. A recent sales catalog from Sears shows their better/best faucets. The "better" faucets — whether for bath vanity or kitchen sink — cost $30 each. Their "best" faucets cost just twice that amount, or $60 each. If you choose the cheaper faucets, which have five-year guarantees, four faucets cost $120. If you choose "best" faucets, which have ten-year guarantees, they will cost $240, or twice the cost of the cheaper models. For $30 per faucet more, you buy the best models available with double the guarantee. Conversely, if you buy the cheaper models, and they perform only for the guarantee period, you'll have leaking

faucets, or face replacement, in a short time. Always consider the expected lifespan, plus frequency of repair, plus extra features when you buy building materials.

## EXTERIOR MATERIALS

### Roofing Materials

Great strides have been made in roofing materials over the past twenty years. When I started in the building trades, the life expectancy of asphalt shingles was normally ten to fifteen years. Today, thanks to improved base mats using fiberglass rather than paper, the warranty on asphalt shingles can be for thirty years or more. Ceramic granules, used to help the shingle resist direct ultraviolet rays from the sun, have replaced the old gravel granules. Not only has the shingle gained an extended lifespan, asphalt shingles that have deep shadow lines or thick butt edges are much more attractive than the roofing of even twenty years ago. Also noted has been a great increase in the variety of colors and tones available, so shingles can provide striking complementary accents with the color of the house siding. Consider that today you can finance a new house with a thirty-year mortgage, with no replacement roofing costs for the lifetime of the mortgage.

### Siding

If you monitor the home buyer surveys that the National Association of Home Builders (NAHB) conducts annually, you will see that the enduring siding choice of upper bracket buyers is consistently masonry, either stone or brick. Small wonder: Masonry exteriors bespeak permanence, richness, and enduring value. Masonry requires almost no maintenance and will stand for centuries if properly executed. Business executives, who are used to making business decisions on the basis of "life cycle costing" — considering initial cost, total maintenance, and the lifespan of the product — make the same search for quality when building their homes. You don't have to paint stone or brick every five to seven years, plus masonry is much more attractive to most buyers. So, if you want to choose a low-maintenance exterior for your barrier-free home, choose masonry.

Next in line for low maintenance are the man-made sidings of metal or vinyl. These prefinished materials often carry warranties of twenty-five years or more and require no paint maintenance for many years. In truth, any product that is painted will ultimately lose the paint coat and require repainting. But metal or vinyl siding can usually buy you a twenty to twenty-five year hiatus from painting costs. If you choose aluminum or vinyl rain gutters and soffit/fascia finish, you can make your entire exterior maintenance free.

## WINDOWS

Since the energy guidelines for windows were established during the last oil crisis, window construction has become an art. New weatherstripping techniques, glass that reflects heat back to the direction from which it comes (called low-E for low emissivity) for better energy efficiency, plus exterior cladding of aluminum or vinyl for no warp, no rot, and no maintenance service all provide good reason to choose the best windows available if building new and for replacing old windows if you are remodeling. Buy casement-type windows that can be operated by crank or lever, test the smooth operation of these new models and compare it to the old double-hung models you now have, and you will quickly conclude they are worth the cost difference.

## DOORS

If your present house is more than ten years old, check out the entry doors. Quite likely you will find peeling paint, splits in the wood rails, damaged or missing weatherstripping, a door that is warped, sagged, or loose on the hinges. If you have one of these older doors you probably also have a combination or "storm" door, so even if your doors were attractive you couldn't see them.

By contrast, modern doors are available with steel skins and foam insulation cores or with fiberglass and a foam insulation core. The doors have magnetic weatherstrip, the same type of weatherstrip or seal used on refrigerator doors, for complete draft-free operation. With the foam insulation core the door is about 1½ times as energy efficient as your old door-plus-storm-door pair, and because there is no secondary door the primary door is revealed in all its beauty. The doors can be trimmed with attractive moldings. Some have wood grain finish, and the fiberglass doors can be stained to look like real wood. Check out such name brands as Pease and Therma-Tru when you shop for a door that will never warp or stick and seldom or never need refinishing.

If you throw in such accents as fiberglass window shutters that never warp or peel and never need painting (well, never is a long time; make that *seldom* need painting), you have achieved an exterior that will be maintenance free for at least twenty-five years, perhaps longer.

## INTERIORS

Interior materials, too, can be bought with wearability that makes them almost bulletproof. From floor covering to appliances, select products that will keep repairmen as lonely as the advertised Maytag man. Again, we urge that you subscribe to *Consumer Reports* magazine and send for their reprints of product test comparisons. These reports may surprise you when you find that the most expensive or best-known brand or model may not be highly rated when compared to its peers. For example, I recall one comparison test of vacuum cleaners in which the winner was a medium-priced model, made by a Japanese manufacturer, one I would not have thought of had I gone shopping for a vacuum cleaner. For subscription information, write to:

*Consumer Reports*
Subscription Department
Box 51166
Boulder, CO 80321-1166

Conventional advice for carpeting is to buy a heavy-duty carpet and install a thick pad under it. Not only does the thicker carpet feel more luxurious, the thicker material provides a cushion against shock between the foot and the floor underlayment. For barrier-free living, however, we urge you to buy a carpet with low-level fiber, installed with a ¼-inch thick commercial pad. This combination provides much more secure footing for those who are unsteady on foot. As mentioned in the chapter on stairs, we prefer no carpet at all for stairs: if the occupant will settle for nothing less, then we again urge low-level fiber and thin commercial pad for maximum security against falling.

For the unsteady or infirm, carpets that resist staining are a precaution against inevitable spills. Check out brands such as Stainmaster by DuPont that provide easy cleaning and resistance to lasting stains in the carpet.

No-wax or shiny vinyl floor covering can also provide low maintenance wear, although you will notice that most makers of home care products offer a treatment product for what are supposed to be no-wax floorings. As a practical matter, most flooring experts I have talked with recommend a quality wax as a protection against scratching and finish wear, even on wood floors. Resist, however, the urge to protect floors with throw rugs. The throw rugs can slide on hard-finish flooring, resulting in a nasty fall and potentially major injury.

## PANELING

Wood paneling can offer lasting beauty, low maintenance, and good resistance to damage from passing traffic. Paneling is especially useful when applied to walls in stairways, entries, or halls where there is a lot of traffic. If you are installing the thinner ³⁄₁₆-inch thick decorative panels, be sure to install a backer board of wallboard, at least ³⁄₈-inch thick, to make the wall more impact-resistant. Paneling can provide years of maintenance-free service. If wood tones make a hall too dark, consider installing paneling only 4 feet high on the wall, wainscot style, to protect the lower portion of the wall. If a wheelchair or walker will be used in the dining area, a wainscot of wood, at least 32 inches high from the floor, can protect wallboard against damage and stains.

## WALL COVERING

Heavy-duty vinyl wall covering can also provide years of low-maintenance protection, while offering pattern and texture to the decorating scheme.

My first exposure to one particular brand, Sanitas, came many years ago when I was in the decorating business. The homeowner wanted his kitchen stripped down to bare plaster, cracked plaster repaired, and the room redecorated. The Sanitas wall covering was some fifteen years old and still as clean as the day it was installed. When I started to strip it, I pulled a corner and the entire sheet peeled free with no problem. I had the stuff off the walls and on the floor in perhaps thirty minutes. If you'd like that kind of long-term washability with easy removal when the time comes, contact:

Sanitas Wallcoverings
170 North Main Street
Wharton, NJ 07885
(201) 361-3800

Most vinyl wall coverings today are strippable and easy to hang. Some coverings have a paper backing, permitting you to peel off the vinyl sheet, then soak the paper backing off the wall. Some solid vinyls peel completely away, and you must remove only the adhesive residue. Because today's wall coverings are often pre-pasted, they leave only minor amounts of adhesive residue when they are removed.

## PAINT

You can judge the washability of paint by checking its sheen: the higher the paint gloss, the better sealed and more washable the surface. Again, *Consumer Reports* does frequent tests on paint to gauge quality. As a general rule you can figure that you don't always get what you pay for, but you never get *more* than you pay for. Shop the name brands and keep an eye on warranties.

The most washable paints are alkyd or oil base high-gloss enamels. Use them wherever moisture is a problem, in kitchens and above ceramic tile or fiberglass tub or shower enclosures. Also, high gloss paints are a plus for traffic routes such as hallways, stairways, and entries. If you have a finished attached garage, a high gloss white enamel will not only look good and be easy to clean, it will reflect light and make the space brighter.

## APPLIANCES

Service charges for repairmen are becoming astronomical, and those service calls can especially upset the budget of the elderly or those on a fixed income. It is much better to buy the best appliances, with low frequency of repairs, than to buy the cheaper brand and be stuck for the repair bills. A one hundred dollar savings on an appliance will disappear with the first service call, and you are still stuck with the lesser brand. Check the EER labels (energy efficiency rating) to try and assess the actual cost of operating the appliance. Remember that the true cost of any product is computed by taking Initial cost – Repair costs – Operating costs, divided by the life expectancy in years. Thus a clothes washer that has a $500 initial cost, plus an annual operating cost of $25 x 10 years (life expectancy) = $250, plus total repairs of $250 costs $1,000 for ten years' operation, or $100 per year actual cost. Higher operating and repair costs can very quickly offset the low initial cost of a cheaper machine.

Beyond the dollar cost of owning and operating appliances is the convenience factor. Waiting for repairmen and the inconvenience of being without needed appliances can also create a frustration factor that cannot be measured in dollars but can be a real problem for the elderly or less able. Many manufacturers seem to think we should be satisfied if they do repairs on a warranty basis. Rather than free repairs, I prefer quality machinery that can be depended upon.

## LIGHT BULBS

With recent emphasis on energy conservation you have no doubt heard that fluorescent lights are cheaper and longer lasting than incandescent bulbs. I have also seen fluorescent bulbs that can be substituted in light fixtures or lamp sockets to replace incandescent bulbs. But there are long-life incandescent bulbs that are built for commercial and industrial use, bulbs that far outlast the bulbs we buy in retail outlets. One bulb we know of is said to last about twenty-six times as long as incandescent bulbs, or 20,000 hours. The bulbs are available in 75 or 100 watts, either clear or frosted, and they sell for $18.95 for a pack of six bulbs, or about $3.15 per bulb. Aside from being cheaper to use then ordinary incandescent bulbs, the less able will not have to fuss about with changing the bulbs. We feel they are particularly needed for ceiling light fixtures, or for lights that require even higher ladders to reach, such as in the top of a stairwell or high up in a garage. They are good insurance against frequent burnout in a sickroom, or for use where there is frequent night traffic such as in the center hall or bath. For information contact:

Gardener's Supply
128 Intervale Road
Burlington, VT 05401
(802) 863-1700

# Life Expectancies of Various Parts of the House

| Item | Useful Life | Remarks |
| --- | --- | --- |
| **Footings and foundations** | | |
| Footings | life | First three items are likely to last up to 250 |
| Foundation | life | years. There are homes in the United |
| Concrete block | life | States over 300 years old. Structural defects |
| Waterproofing: | | that do develop are a result of poor soil |
|    Bituminous coating | 5 years | conditions. |
|    Pargeting with Ionite | life | |
| Termite-proofing | 5 years | Maybe earlier in damp climates. |
| Gravel outside | 30-40 years | Depends on usage. |
| Cement block | life | Less strong than concrete block. |
| | | |
| **Rough structure** | | |
| Floor system (basement) | life | |
| Framing exterior walls | life | Usually plaster directly on masonry. Plaster is solid and will last forever. Provides tighter seal than drywall and better insulation. |
| | | |
| Framing interior walls | life | In older homes, usually plaster on wood lath. Lath strips lose resilience, causing waves in ceilings and walls. |
| | | |
| **Concrete work:** | | |
| Slab | life | (200 years) |
| Precast decks | 10-15 years | |
| Precast porches | 10-15 years | |
| Site-built porches and steps | 20 years | |
| | | |
| **Sheet metal** | | |
| Gutter, downspouts, and flashing: | | |
|    Aluminum | 20-30 years | Never requires painting, but dents and pits. May need to be replaced sooner for appearance. |
|    Copper | life | Very durable and expensive. Requires regular cleaning and alignment. |
|    Galvanized iron | 15-25 years | Rusts easily and must be kept painted every 3 to 4 years. |

| Item | Useful Life | Remarks |
|---|---|---|
| **Rough electrical** | | |
| Wiring: | | |
| Copper | life | |
| Aluminum | life | |
| Romex | life | |
| Circuit-breaker | | |
| Breaker panel | 30-40 years | |
| Individual breaker | 25-30 years | |
| **Rough plumbing** | | |
| Pressure pipes: | | |
| Copper | life | Strongest and most common. Needs no maintenance. |
| Galvanized iron | 30-50 years | Rusts easily and is major expense in older homes. Most common until 1940. |
| Plastic | 30-40 years | |
| Waste pipe: | | |
| Concrete | 20 years | |
| Vitreous china | 25-30 years | |
| Plastic | 50-70 years | Usage depends upon soil conditions. Acid soils can eat through plastic. |
| Cast iron | life | |
| Lead | life | A leak cannot be patched. If bathroom is remodeled, lead must be replaced. |
| **Heating and venting** | | |
| Duct work: | | |
| Galvanized | 50-70 years | |
| Plastic | 40-60 years | Type used depends upon climate. |
| Fiberglass | 40-60 years | |
| AC rough-in | | Same as Duct work |
| **Roof** | | |
| Asphalt shingles | 15-25 years | Most common. Deterioration subject to climate. Granules come off shingles. Check downspouts. |
| Wood shingles and shakes | 30-40 years | Expensive. Contracts and expands due to climate. |
| Tile | 30-50 years | Tendency to crack on sides. |
| Slate | life | High quality. Maintenance every 2 to 3 years as nails rust. |
| Metal | life | Shorter life if allowed to rust. |
| Built-up asphalt | 20-30 years | Maintenance required — esp. after winter |

| Item | Useful Life | Remarks |
|---|---|---|
| **Roof, cont'd** | | |
| Felt | 30-40 years | |
| Tar and gravel | 10-15 years | |
| Asbestos shingle | 30-40 years | Shingles get brittle when walked on. Maintenance every 1 to 3 years. |
| Composition shingles | 12-16 years | |
| Tin | life | Will rust easily if not kept painted regularly. Found a lot in inner-city row houses. |
| 4 or 5 built-up ply | 15-25 years | Layers of tar paper on tar. |
| **Masonry** | | |
| Chimney | life | |
| Fireplace | 20-30 years | |
| Fire brick | life | |
| Ash dump | life | |
| Metal fireplace | life | |
| Flue tile | life | |
| Brick veneer | life | Joints must be pointed every 5 to 6 years. |
| Brick | life | |
| Stone | life | Unless a porous grade stone like limestone. |
| Block wall | life | |
| Masonry floors | life | Must be kept waxed every 1 to 2 years. |
| Stucco | life | Requires painting every 8 to 10 years. More susceptible to cracking than brick. Replacement is expensive. Maintenance cycles for all types of masonry structures, including those found in urban areas, subjected to dirt, soot, and chemicals: Caulking — every 20 years Pointing — every 35 years Sandblasting — every 35 years |
| **Windows and doors** | | |
| Window glazing | 5-6 years | |
| Storm windows and gaskets | life | Aluminum and wood. |
| Screen doors | 5-8 years | |
| Storm doors | 10-15 years | |
| Interior doors (lauan) | 10 years | |
| Sliding doors | 30-50 years | |
| Folding doors | 30-40 years | |
| Sliding screens | 30 years | |

| Item | Useful Life | Remarks |
|---|---|---|
| **Windows and doors, cont'd** | | |
| Garage doors | 20-25 years | Depends upon initial placement of springs, tracks, and rollers. |
| Steel casement windows | 40-50 years | Have leakage and condensation problems. Installed mostly in 1940s and 1950s. |
| Wood casement windows | 40-50 years | Older types very drafty. |
| Jalousie | 30-40 years | Fair quality available in wood and aluminum. Used mostly for porches. |
| Wood double-hung windows | 40-50 years | |
| **Insulation** | | |
| Foundation | life | |
| Roof, ceiling | life | |
| Roof -- electric vent -- automatic | 10-15 years | |
| Walls | life | |
| Floor | life | |
| Weatherstripping: | | |
| Metal | 8-9 years | |
| Plastic gasket | 5-8 years | |
| **Exterior trim** | | |
| Wood siding | life | Must be kept painted regularly -- every 5-7 years. |
| Metal siding | life | May rust due to climate. |
| Aluminum siding | life | Maintenance free if baked-on finish. |
| Shutters: | | |
| Wood | 20 years | |
| Metal | 20-30 years | |
| Plastic | life | |
| Aluminum | life | |
| Posts and columns | life | |
| Gable vents: | | |
| Wood | 10-14 years | |
| Aluminum | life | |
| Gable vent screens | Same as gable vents | |
| Cornice and rake trim | life | |
| Trellis | 20 years | Will rot in back even if painted because of moisture. |
| **Exterior paint** | | |
| Wood | 3-4 years | Climate a strong factor. |
| Brick | 3-4 years | |
| Aluminum | 10-12 years | |

| Item | Useful Life | Remarks |
|---|---|---|
| **Exterior paint, cont'd** | | |
| Gutters, downspouts, and flashing: | | |
| Aluminum | 10-12 years | |
| Copper | life | No painting required. |
| **Stairs** | | |
| Stringer | 50 years | |
| Risers | 50 years | |
| Treads | 50 years | |
| Baluster | 50 years | |
| Rails | 30-40 years | |
| Starting levels | 50 years | |
| Disappearing stairs | 30-40 years | |
| **Drywall and plaster** | | |
| Drywall | 40-50 years | Lifetime is adequately protected by exterior walls and roof. Cracks must be regularly spackled. |
| Plaster | life | Thicker and more durable than drywall. Exterior must be properly maintained. |
| Ceiling suspension | life | |
| Acoustical ceiling | life | |
| Luminous ceiling | 10-20 years | Discolors easily. |
| **Ceramic tile** | | |
| Tub alcove and shower stall | life | Proper installation and maintenance required for long life. Cracks appear due to moisture and joints; must be grouted every 3-4 years. |
| Bath wainscote | life | |
| Ceramic floor | life | |
| Ceramic tile | life | |
| **Finish carpentry** | | |
| Baseboard and shoe | 40-50 years | |
| Door and window trim | 40-50 years | |
| Wood paneling | 40-50 years | |
| Closet shelves | 40-50 years | |
| Fireplace mantel | 30-40 years | |
| **Flooring** | | |
| Oak floor | life | In most older homes, first story floor is oak; second and third story floors are hard pine. |
| Pine floor | life | |
| Slate flagstone floor | 40-50 years | |
| Resilient (vinyl) | 10-15 years | Because of scuffing may have to be replaced earlier. |
| Terrazzo | life | |
| Carpeting | 5-8 years | Standard carpeting. |

| Item | Useful Life | Remarks |
|---|---|---|
| **Cabinets and vanities** | | |
| Kitchen cabinets | 18-30 years | |
| Bath vanities | 18-30 years | |
| Countertop | 18-30 years | |
| Medicine cabinets | 15-20 years | |
| Mirrors | 10-15 years | |
| Tub enclosures | 18-25 years | |
| Shower doors | 18-25 years | |
| Bookshelves | life | Depends on wood used. |
| **Interior painting** | | |
| Wall paint | 3-5 years | |
| Trim and door | 3-5 years | |
| Wallpaper | 3-7 years | |
| **Electrical finish** | | |
| Electric range and oven | 12-20 years | |
| Vent hood | 15-20 years | |
| Disposal | 5-12 years | |
| Exhaust fan | 8-10 years | |
| Water heater | 10-12 years | |
| Electric fixtures | 20-30 years | |
| Doorbell and chimes | 8-10 years | |
| Fluorescent bulbs | 3-5 years | |
| **Plumbing finish** | | |
| Dishwasher | 5-15 years | |
| Gas water heater | 8-12 years | |
| Gas refrigerator | 15-25 years | |
| Toilet seats | 8-10 years | |
| Commode | 15-25 years | |
| Steel sinks | 15-20 years | |
| China sinks | 15-20 years | |
| Faucets | life | Washers must be replaced frequently. |
| Flush valves | 18-25 years | |
| Well and septic system | 15-30 years | Depends on soil and rock formations. |
| Hot water boilers | 30-50 years | Becomes increasingly inefficient with age and may have to be replaced before it actually breaks down. |
| **Heating finish** | | |
| Wall heaters | 12-17 years | |
| Warm air furnaces | 25-30 years | Most common today. |

| Item | Useful Life | Remarks |
|---|---|---|
| **Heating finish, cont'd** | | |
| Radiant heating: | | |
|     Ceiling | 20-30 years | |
|     Baseboard | 20-40 years | |
| AC unit | 8-18 years | |
| AC compressors | 10-18 years | Regular maintenance required. |
| Humidifier | 7-8 years | |
| Electric air cleaners | 8-10 years | |
| **Appliances** | | |
| Refrigerator | 15-25 years | |
| Washer | 8-12 years | |
| Dryer | 8-12 years | |
| Combo washer and dryer | 7-10 years | |
| Garage door opener | 8-10 years | |
| Disposal units | 8-12 years | |
| Dishwasher | 8-12 years | |
| Lawn mower | 7-10 years | Must be serviced regularly. |
| Vacuum cleaner | 6-10 years | |
| Music system (intercom) | 30-40 years | |
| **Appointments** | | |
| Closet rods | life | |
| Blinds | 10-15 years | |
| Drapes | 5-10 years | |
| Towel bars | 10-15 years | |
| Soap grab | 10-12 years | |
| **Others** | | |
| Fences and screens | 20-30 years | |
| Splash blocks | 6-7 years | |
| Patios (concrete) | 15-50 years | |
| Gravel walks | 3-5 years | |
| Concrete walks | 10-25 years | |
| Sprinkler system | 15-25 years | |
| Asphalt driveway | 5-6 years | With patchwork may last 15-20 years. |
| Tennis court | 20-40 years | |

The chart above was compiled by Dean Christ and is used here courtesy of the Economics Division, National Association of Home Builders.

# 9
# Choosing a Lot and Hiring a Contractor

Choosing a building lot becomes more difficult if you are planning a barrier-free house. Obviously, any lot, whatever the grade, could be a candidate for this house, assuming you would want to bulldoze the actual house site and the area immediately around it to make it easily accessible. But other factors than just than the grade are important in choosing the site for a barrier-free house.

Things to keep in mind when shopping for a barrier-free site include the following:

❑ Is there public transportation nearby, in the event that the handicapped or less able person may need a hired companion?

❑ Is the site close to medical and shopping facilities?

❑ Is the site close to emergency services such as hospital or ambulance service?

❑ Is there a nearby pharmacy?

❑ Is there a church or synagogue within easy traveling distance?

❑ Is there a sunny exposure to build a deck or patio where a housebound person could enjoy the sun and fresh air?

❑ Would the driveway slope to the south or west, so that solar rays would keep the drive and entry walk ice-free in winter?

❑ Will the house be near a park or nature walk, for the enjoyment of the less able?

❑ What particular individual needs must be met for the person or persons involved? Try to anticipate any drawbacks before you make a final decision.

## HIRING A CONTRACTOR

Having been in the building business, we have often been asked: "How can I find a reputable contractor?" I am both wearied and offended by oft-repeated advice to hire a contractor, assume he is a crook, then treat him like the thief he is. My own advice would be to spend some time choosing this important person, ask for references, and check him out. Then proceed on the premise that you have hired a reputable person and trust him to do the job you are paying him for.

Premise #1: A consultant, realtor, architect, or builder should save you more than the cost of his or her services. It is wisely observed that he who acts as his own lawyer has a fool for a client, and in my opinion the same observation goes for he who acts as his own builder. To everything, including building, there is a season, and the builder must schedule the trades in a particular order or waste and conflict — perhaps even chaos — may result. If you don't know the rational procedures of how a house goes together, hire someone who does know. Expect him to earn his money.

Next: Unless his name is Frank Lloyd Wright, or another name as familiar in building, hire someone local. You will want the person handy when decisions are to be made, when unexpected downpours wash out the freshly poured foundations, when the plumbing contractor doesn't show up, and when the house is to be occupied, or would be occupied if you could get the sticking door open. Hire someone who builds in the area in which he lives, who faces his customers daily on his rounds.

When hiring the local builder or contractor, check with the local office of the National Association of Home Builders (NAHB) or the National Association of the Remodeling Industry (NARI). These organizations represent professionals who try to police their own industry. They have codes of ethics, standards for membership, and review or appeals panels for the customer. The organizations screen members for you.

Ask for a contractor who has barrier-free building experience. What you need here is people who are aware of the options available, who can help plan the house so there are no design errors to haunt and frustrate you later. Ask for job references, visit the job sites, and talk to the customers.

Also, ask for credit references. Check with the bank references, subcontractors the contractor uses, material suppliers he buys from, realtors who have sold his houses. The time to be wary is before you sign the papers.

Have several sets of plans and several copies of the spec sheet. The spec sheet is short for "specifications" and lists by model or brand name the materials that will be used. This ensures that there is no apples-and-oranges bidding. The spec sheet makes sure that every bidder is bidding to build the same house, using the same materials.

## Getting Bids

When you have solicited bids from several legitimate contractors, compare the bids. Is there wide disagreement over the price? If you have been impressed with a particular builder thus far, but his bid seems out of line, ask him to explain the bid. Is he promising something the others are not? Are all bidders licensed, bonded, and insured to protect you? Don't let a discrepancy in the bids cause you to act hastily. Find out the reason the bids are far apart, if such is the case.

Also, don't necessarily accept the low bidder. If any other bidder seemed more to your liking, and bid prices are within, say, 10 percent, that small difference can buy you a lot of peace of mind. If you are feeling a growing sense of confidence in one bidder, hire him.

## Making the Choice

What kind of person do you want to hire? Let me illustrate. I was maybe fourteen years old, working in the summer with my father, helping on a housing project. I started to hang a wallboard panel and my father said: "Wait a minute. There is no backing in that corner." I replied: "Who is going to know?" My father looked at me quizzically and replied: "Why, I am." That's the kind of person you want to hire.

When you have chosen your builder, ask for a detailed contract. Get everything in writing. Count on nothing that is verbal or implied. There is nothing that will sour a building relationship quicker than misunderstanding. I am absolutely convinced that there are more deals ruined by misunderstanding and miscommunication than by fraud. Be very sure both you and the contractor understand exactly what is expected, and you will avoid much frustration.

Be specific about your needs *before* construction starts. Your builder needs to know exactly what you want, not just "place the tub faucets at a convenient height" but the exact height you will need. It is helpful to supply brand names and manufacturers' names whenever possible, especially in the case of unusual equipment.

During the construction period, keep an eye on your house as it grows. If you see anything that looks wrong or is not as you expected, ask questions. Most errors are easy to correct if caught early enough; even changes in the plan may be minor, if the change is made before you are too far along with the original plan.

# 10
# Adaptable Plans

Following World War II, there was a growing need for housing that would be accessible to handicapped people. Injured war veterans, victims of the polio epidemics of the '40s and '50s, a growing population and injuries from accidents in the growing fleet of personal automobiles all contributed to the demand for accessible housing. Add to these the fact of an aging general population and you can see a skyrocketing need to make housing as accessible as possible.

In 1961 the American National Standards Institute (ANSI) published "Specifications for Making Buildings and Facilities Accessible to, and Usable by, the Physically Handicapped." The standards were a good first effort, but they did not completely cover all types of disabilities.

In 1984 the ANSI technical specifications were combined into the "Uniform Federal Accessibility Standards" (UFAS) and became the current standard for uniformity in federal and private construction systems.

State and local governments in the past often dictated that a certain percentage — usually 5 to 10 percent — of multi-family housing should offer "fixed accessibility." This meant the builder had to provide a small number of housing units that were specially designed to meet special needs. But this system of building housing of special design, and

in low numbers, did not satisfy the housing needs of the less able.

The flaws in the system were failures that affected both the builders and the less able. From the builders' viewpoint, the accessible rental units looked too institutional, so only the less able, who needed the special features, would rent them. The builders often could not make a profit or recover their investments for special items. Fully able tenants were not willing to lose the base cabinet space that was traded for under-counter knee space. Builders often lowered the rent to attract the non-disabled people and thus lost money on the deals.

For the handicapped who needed the housing, rental fees often exceeded the budget. Often, the fixed-accessible units had only a single bedroom, and thus could not be used by a family. The units were spotted randomly in new apartment construction, often in suburbs that lacked public transportation. The less able were forced to live not where they would choose but wherever the units were available. Plus, the standards applied only to new construction, so this compounded the problems of location and affordability.

No one was really happy with the situation. Apartment owners lobbied to have the mandatory percentages of "fixed accessible" units eliminated

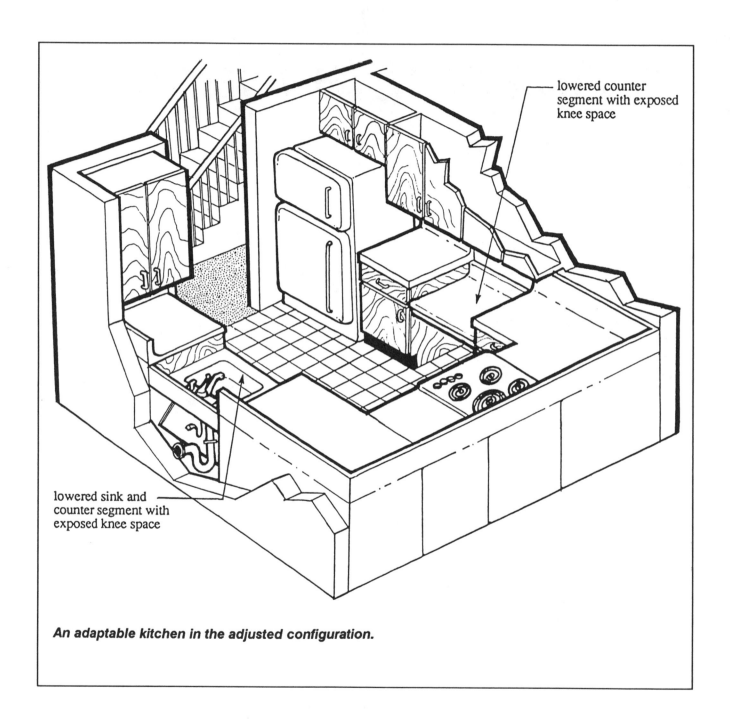

lowered counter
segment with exposed
knee space

lowered sink and
counter segment with
exposed knee space

*An adaptable kitchen in the adjusted configuration.*

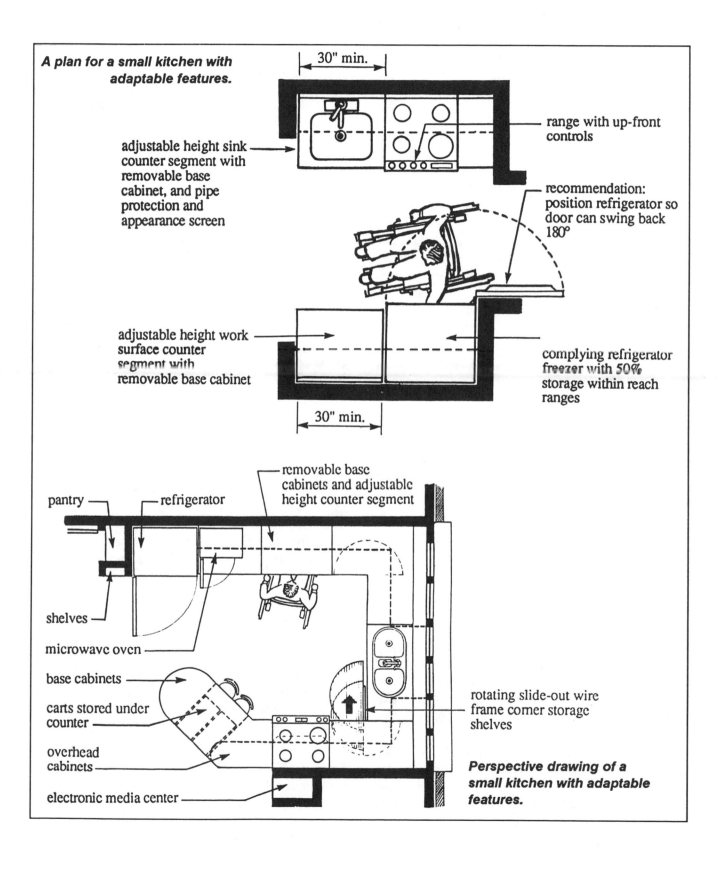

**A plan for a small kitchen with adaptable features.**

30" min.

adjustable height sink counter segment with removable base cabinet, and pipe protection and appearance screen

range with up-front controls

recommendation: position refrigerator so door can swing back 180°

adjustable height work surface counter segment with removable base cabinet

complying refrigerator freezer with 50% storage within reach ranges

30" min.

pantry

refrigerator

removable base cabinets and adjustable height counter segment

shelves

microwave oven

base cabinets

carts stored under counter

overhead cabinets

electronic media center

rotating slide-out wire frame corner storage shelves

**Perspective drawing of a small kitchen with adaptable features.**

or cut back. The less able population continued to feel the frustrations of finding suitable housing. From this dual discontent emerged the concept of adaptable housing.

By definition, an adaptable housing unit is one that avoids the appearance of a "special institutional look" while meeting the needs of the less able by adding or adjusting certain elements. Adaptable house units incorporate all the features required by ANSI and UFAS — wider doors, clear floor space, accessible routes — and permit a choice on certain adjustable or fixed features. Several states have incorporated adaptable concepts in their building codes, as an alternative to the fixed accessible approach of the past.

## PRINCIPAL ELEMENTS OF ADAPTABLE HOUSING

There are three principal elements of adaptable housing. They are:

1. Removable base cabinets and bath vanities that can be removed for knee space if necessary. The cabinets offer more storage plus a standard appearance for the non-disabled.

2. Segments of countertops that can be adjusted from the standard 36-inch height down to 28 inches for the less able.

3. Reinforced wall areas to support grab bars where needed.

Adaptable homes are fully accessible, and the special features are not obvious. Such homes are attractive, functional, and competitively priced when they are properly done. Note that these principles make the house truly adaptable without renovation, by adjustment or adapting only, because the basics are already a part of the unit. To adapt the housing units, one must remove cabinets or vanities to reveal the knee space under the work surface, adjust countertop and sink heights

in bathroom and kitchen, and add grab bars as needed for support. Other changes might include lowering heights of desk tops, work surfaces in a shop or utility room, or lowered counters in the laundry.

Fixed accessible features, which are structural and must be combined with the adjustable features, include wide doors, no entrance steps, light switches and controls that are mounted low, and rooms and spaces located along an accessible route such as a great room or wider halls. Options not mentioned in the standards might also include alarms for people who are hearing-impaired and adjustable storage areas.

## BENEFITS OF ADAPTABLE HOUSING

There are benefits in adaptable housing for developers and owners, as well as for the less able. The units can be rented — or sold — to either the less able or the unimpaired. This will expand the rental market or increase the market for resale. Low counters appeal to shorter people as well as to the less able. There is less damage to walls and doors when furniture is moved through wider halls or doorways. Increased floor space in the bathroom lets the occupant "decorate" with shelves or other furnishings, and the larger bathroom has universal appeal.

Adaptable housing also permits us to remain in place longer. The less able won't move so often if they find a place that "fits"; the non-disabled will not have to move if they become infirm or disabled as they age. Aging persons tend to reject the amenities that might suggest they need "special" housing but will welcome them as they become needed.

Most housing can be made adaptable at little or no increased cost. For those who currently have no need of special equipment, accessible housing is a blessing to less able visitors and guests. The move to accessible/adaptable housing also has opened up a wide market for new products. For example, grab bars were once made solely for institutions, of chrome or stainless steel. Today, a wide variety of grab bars is offered, plastic-coated and in an array of colors to blend with any color of tile or paint. Because there are an estimated 125,000 bath and/or shower accidents annually in the U.S., we think grab bars should be mandatory in these potentially hazardous areas.

Building a new adaptable house may be less costly than you think. In a recent article in *Popular Science* magazine, Liza Bowles, a Vice President of the Research Center of the National Association of Home Builders, said that the cost of building an adaptable, accessible house is only 2 to 3 percent more than that of a standard house.

## COST ESTIMATES FOR ADAPTABLE FEATURES

Studies done by the Department of Housing and Urban Development (HUD) provide us with preliminary cost guidelines for including adaptable features in a house. Costs may vary by location, but the estimates provide a starting point for those planning to build adaptable housing.

### Cabinets and Countertops

For adaptable base cabinets, which can be removed or altered to permit knee space under countertops, HUD estimates that you can substitute a custom cabinet for a stock cabinet for an additional 80 percent expenditure. The stock cabinet would be unscrewed from the wall or countertop and removed. The custom cabinet would have a base or floor that folds up against the back of the cabinet, plus double doors that can be folded alongside the sides of the cabinet.

Countertops can be mounted in a fixed position or made adjustable. A section of the countertop can be set on a fixed frame with spacers for about 50 percent higher cost than for standard tops, on movable strips for about 112 percent more than a standard mount, or on adjustable wall mounts for about 137 percent more than the cost for a standard countertop.

### Reinforcing Walls

Reinforcing wall areas to hold grab bars can be done in two ways. The first way is to nail 2 x 10 fir planks between the studs, at the recommended heights. The estimated cost of doing this reinforcement in the area of a 5-foot bathtub is about $15. For a 3' x 3' shower area, fir reinforcing should cost about $10; 2 x 10 reinforcing for the two walls by a toilet would likewise cost about $10.

A second way to reinforce walls to hold grab bars is to cover the entire area with heavy 3/4-inch plywood. This method is slightly more expensive to put together, but offers complete freedom in placing the grab bars because the entire wall area is reinforced. Covering the wall along a 5-foot long bathtub would cost an estimated $45; plywood alongside a toilet would also cost $45, while covering three walls of 3' x 3' shower stall might cost $65.

## POSTING DIRECTIONS

The Uniform Federal Accessibility Standards (UFAS) direct that each adaptable housing unit should be provided with a list of adaptable features, plus instructions for making changes to convert the unit(s). The list should include the height adjustments that can be made for countertops and sinks in the kitchen or bath vanity. Obviously, such a list will be necessary so that new owners and/or occupants are aware of the adaptable features available to them.

The list of adaptable features, and directions for

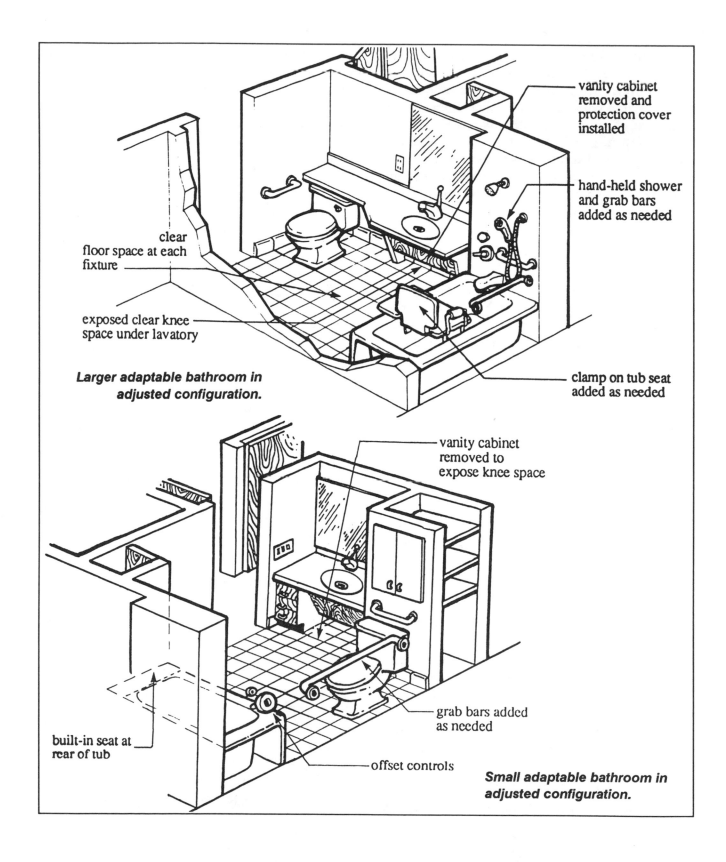

vanity cabinet
removed and
protection cover
installed

hand-held shower
and grab bars
added as needed

clear
floor space at each
fixture

exposed clear knee
space under lavatory

clamp on tub seat
added as needed

**Larger adaptable bathroom in
adjusted configuration.**

vanity cabinet
removed to
expose knee space

built-in seat at
rear of tub

grab bars added
as needed

offset controls

**Small adaptable bathroom in
adjusted configuration.**

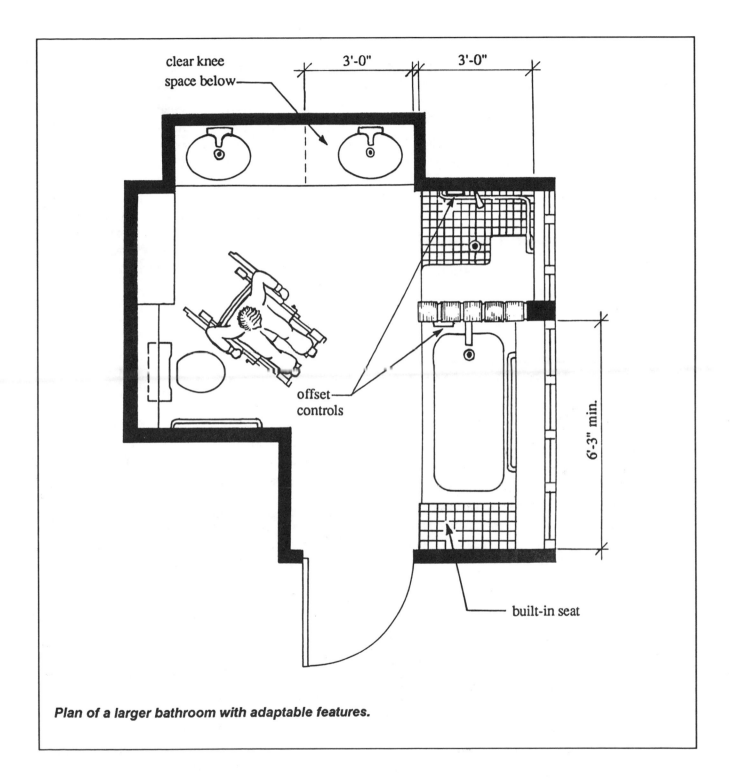

clear knee
space below

3'-0"

3'-0"

offset
controls

6-3" min.

built-in seat

*Plan of a larger bathroom with adaptable features.*

making any changes necessary, can be posted where it will not be removed by unthinking owners or tenants. The list might be displayed inside a cabinet, on the inside of a cabinet door, or on a bulletin board in the laundry or furnace area.

In addition to the permanently posted directions, UFAS specifies that the owner or manager of the building be provided with written and illustrated instruction on how to find and adjust adaptable features.

## THE FUTURE OF ADAPTABLE DESIGN

While there has been an increasing amount of attention paid to making government, public, and multi-unit housing accessible to the less able, there are no mandates for making single housing units more accessible or adaptable.

The building industry, however, is moving on its own to offer more accessible/adaptable design. The subject was very much on the minds of the participants at the 1990 National Association of Home Builders Show (NAHB), held in January 1990 in Atlanta, Georgia. The show homes on the convention floor were accessible, and manufacturers showed a host of new products designed with greater convenience and accessibility.

Barrier-free bathing fixtures, kitchen cabinets mounted on tracks so they were height-adjustable at the push of a button, cabinets with an 8½-inch kick space at the bottom to accommodate the foot platform on a wheelchair (by Merillat Inc.), and temperature-controlled shower and sink faucets were among the products we saw demonstrated.

Almost any single-story home can be adapted for barrier-free living. Two-story homes can be adapted, too, with the inclusion of home elevators or stair lifts (see the Appendix and/or the Yellow Pages under "Elevators — Sales & Service"). To build a house that can later accommodate an elevator, you need only align walk-in closets on each floor. Then, if the need for an elevator arises, the elevator shaft is already in place.

Nor must a house be specifically built for the less able to be barrier-free. Most of the features we've suggested here can be added to an existing house. Indeed, we feel that there is a new industry out there, just waiting for remodelers to convert existing housing to adaptable or barrier-free housing. A study done in Florida showed that the majority of older people are willing to pay extra for such conveniences as easy-access lever door handles, grab bars for support in bathtub and shower, and non-slip flooring.

## REALTORS

Present estimates are that between 20 and 25 percent of American families have a member who is less able. Assuming the statistics are true, houses that have barriers to good accessibility can have a high resistance to resale, because they exclude — automatically — up to one-fourth of all potential home buyers. The savvy real estate firm will have in-house specialists who cater directly to the needs of the less able or elderly. Those who list houses for sale, and the people who create the advertising copy for the classified ads in the newspapers, should be trained to take particular note of the barrier-free features of a house and to mention them in any advertising. Any house with entry ramps instead of steps or grab bars in the bathroom automatically should command extra interest from the less able, who until now have been ignored as a forgotten minority.

If you have a house for sale, and have joined the "FSBO" ranks ("for sale by owner"), it will cost little to install single lever faucets, lever-type door handles, and a grab bar in the bathtub or shower. If you are writing your own newspaper ads or showing your own house, make a list of the features that eliminate barriers — oversize bathroom, no steps at entries, lever-type faucets, intercoms in bedrooms or at the entry — and point them out to prospective buyers. Full accessibility may be the feature that finally convinces a buyer to choose your house over competing houses.

## BUILDING AN ADAPTABLE HOUSE

If you are thinking of building a new house, contact your local office of the NAHB for the name of the builder who has experience in building barrier-free or adaptable housing. Check with your city building department and ask if the planners there have developed guidelines for building barrier-free homes. Also, check around for references to architects who have designed and built housing for the elderly and/or the less able.

There are several ways to approach the question of improved home accessibility. First, there is the direct approach of building a house that is custom-designed to meet the specific needs of yourself or your family members. However, the custom house built just for you may lack resale value if modifications to expensive cabinets and plumbing leave the house with an "institutional" look. The best approach is to consider building an adaptable house which will have the structural accessible features such as wide doors and halls, single-lever faucets and door handles, additional electrical outlets set at a more convenient height from the floor, and countertops of various heights built in. The accessible design is more comfortable for anyone to live in. If you build in the adaptable features listed in this chapter, the house can be changed at a later date to accommodate changing physical needs. For example, removable/folding base cabinets permit you to have the extra convenience of base storage space when it is needed or to remove the base cabinets if under-counter knee space is necessary.

Important, too, is to incorporate any features that reduce or eliminate home maintenance costs. Keep in mind that routine maintenance chores that are do-it-yourself tasks for the fully able become expensive repair jobs that the less able must hire someone to do.

Check with testing organizations such as Consumers Union (publishers of *Consumer Reports*) when buying home appliances or equipment. Consider not only the initial cost of the item but the frequency of repair, to avoid costly repair calls and disruption for the homebound or less able person.

Also choose high efficiency appliances when equipping the new house. Check the EER (energy efficiency rating) when buying appliances, and buy those with the highest rating for energy economy. Low-flow shower heads and mini-flush toilets can easily reduce water consumption by half, with a corresponding reduction in utility bills.

Thus, with a little advance planning we can have a house that follows today's basic designs, but is easily altered to meet changing physical needs. This is particularly desirable in light of an AARP (American Association of Retired Persons) survey which reveals that the great majority of people who are sixty years of age or over prefer to "age in place" — to remain in their own familiar homes, rather than moving to a retirement home or a high-rise apartment building.

In the Appendix (Designs and Plans) we have included plans for new houses of various styles, sizes, and costs. All were architect-designed to be barrier-free for maximum mobility. All are designed to incorporate preplanned flexibility so they can easily be adapted to fit specific needs. The plans shown can be obtained from:

Source I Designers' Network
International Market Square
275 Market Street, Suite 521
Minneapolis, MN 55405
(800) 547-5570

# *Appendix*

### 1.
### Designs and Plans to Accommodate Wheelchair Users

### 2.
### Independent Living Centers

### 3.
### Information Centers

### 4.
### Organizations

### 5.
### Amputee Support Groups

### 6.
### Products

### 7.
### Books

### 8.
### Magazines and Newsletters

### 9.
### Catalogs

# DESIGNS AND PLANS

# TO ACCOMMODATE WHEELCHAIR USERS

## BATHROOMS AND LAVATORIES
### Space Allowances for Wheelchairs

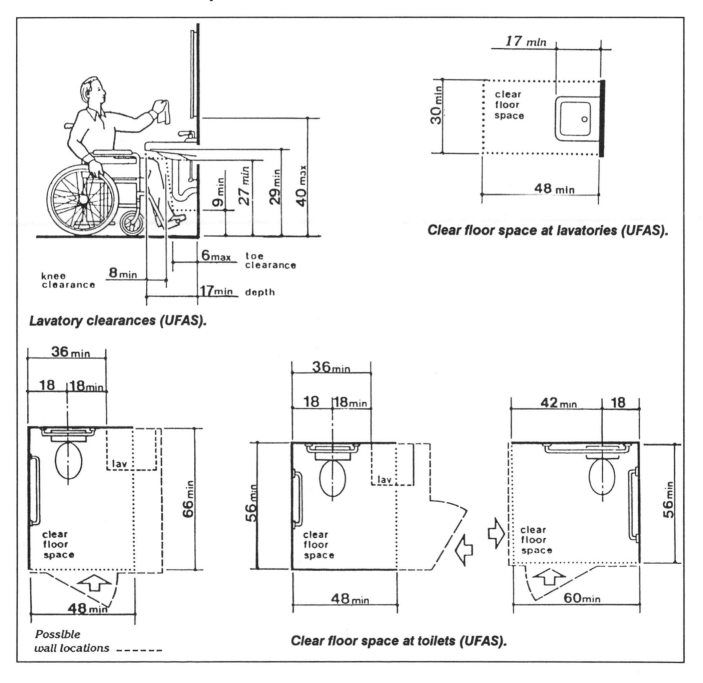

**Lavatory clearances (UFAS).**

**Clear floor space at lavatories (UFAS).**

**Clear floor space at toilets (UFAS).**

Possible wall locations ------

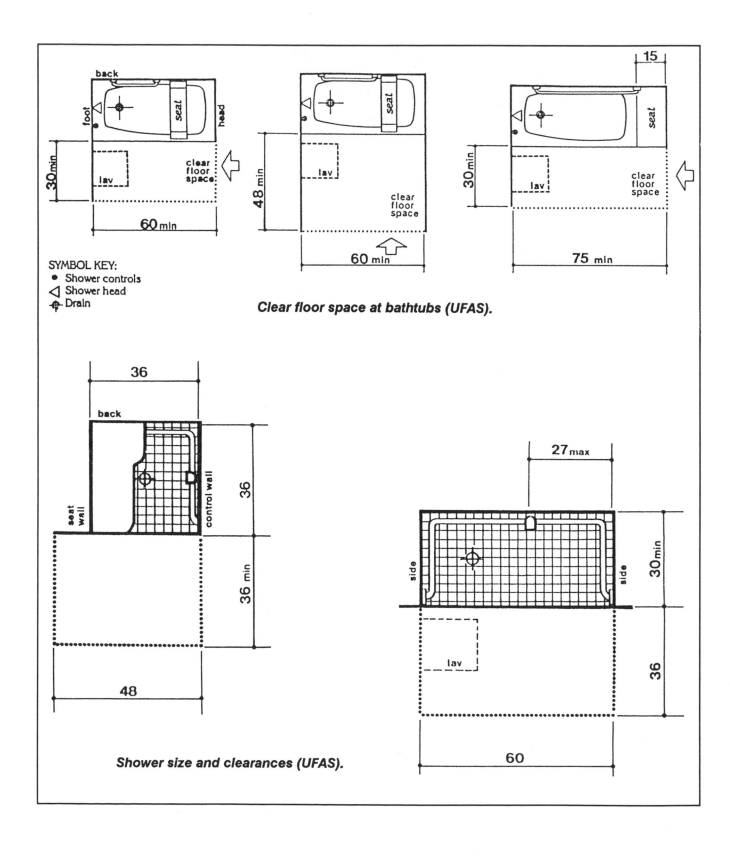

*Clear floor space at bathtubs (UFAS).*

SYMBOL KEY:
● Shower controls
◁ Shower head
⊕ Drain

*Shower size and clearances (UFAS).*

# Toilet and Bathtub Grab Bars

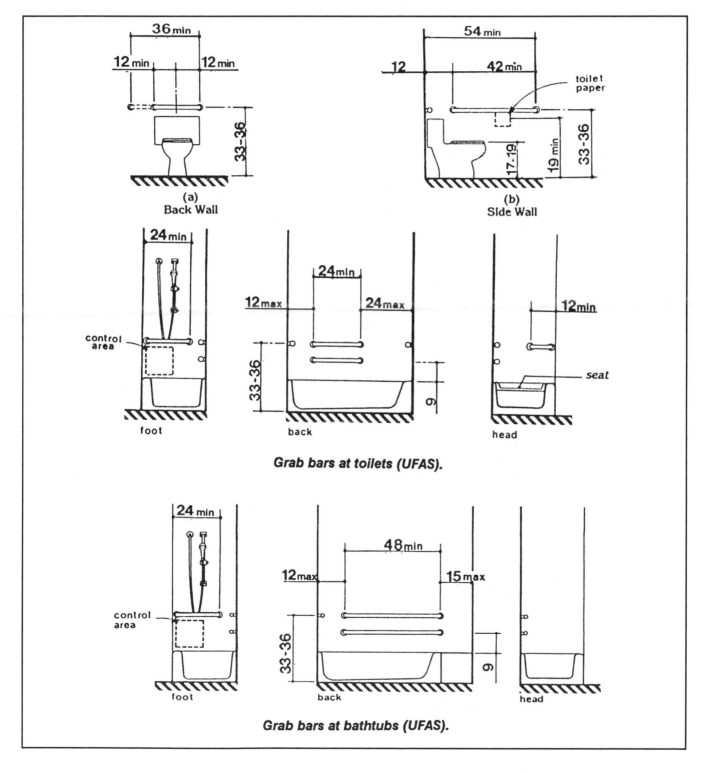

**(a) Back Wall**

**(b) Side Wall**

*Grab bars at toilets (UFAS).*

*Grab bars at bathtubs (UFAS).*

## Adaptable Bath Tub Grab Bars

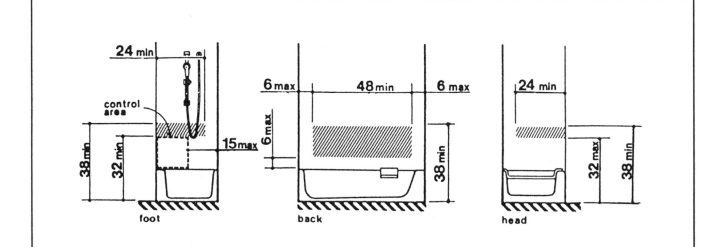

*Location of grab bars and controls of adaptable bathtubs (UFAS).*

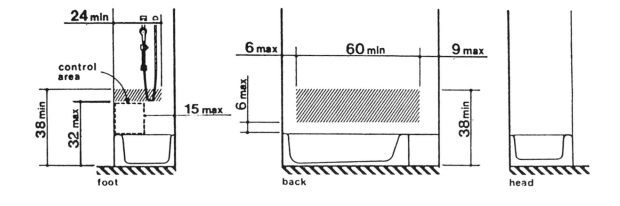

## Table Space Requirements

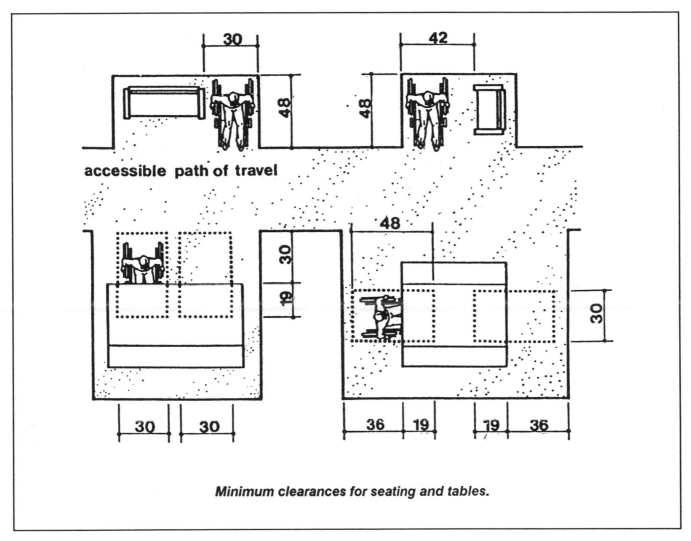

*Minimum clearances for seating and tables.*

# TYPICAL HOMES DESIGNED
# TO ACCOMMODATE WHEELCHAIR USERS

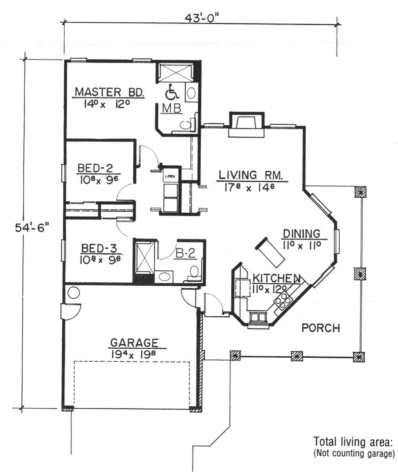

43'-0"

MASTER BD.
14⁰ x 12⁰

MB

BED-2
10⁸ x 9⁶

LINEN

LIVING RM.
17⁸ x 14⁶

54'-6"

DINING
11⁰ x 11⁰

BED-3
10⁸ x 9⁶

B-2

KITCHEN
11⁰ x 12⁸

GARAGE
19⁴ x 19⁸

PORCH

Total living area:             1,307 sq. ft.
(Not counting garage)

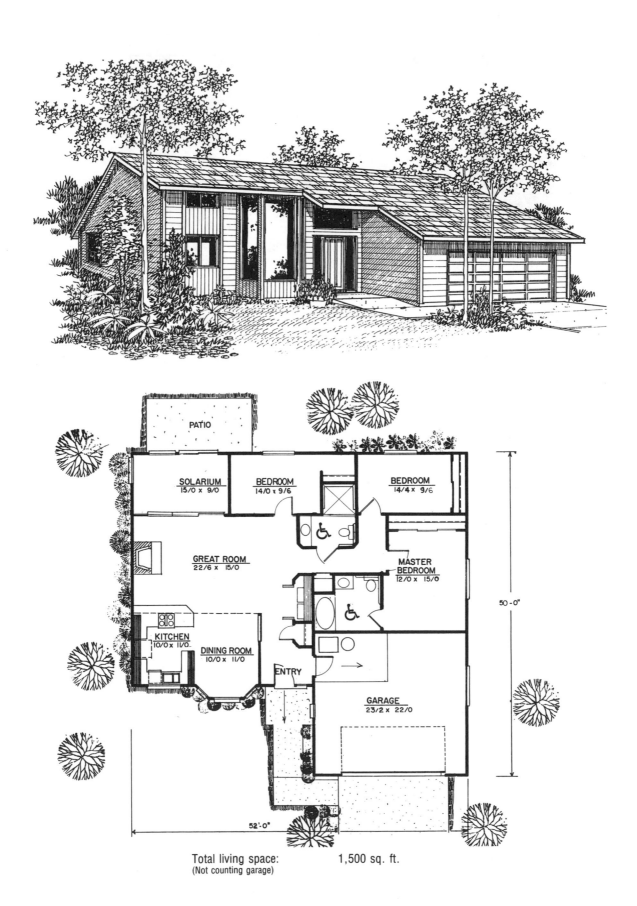

PATIO

SOLARIUM
15/0 x 9/0

BEDROOM
14/0 x 9/6

BEDROOM
14/4 x 9/6

GREAT ROOM
22/6 x 15/0

MASTER
BEDROOM
12/0 x 15/0

KITCHEN
10/0 x 11/0

DINING ROOM
10/0 x 11/0

ENTRY

GARAGE
23/2 x 22/0

50 - 0"

52'-0"

Total living space:          1,500 sq. ft.
(Not counting garage)

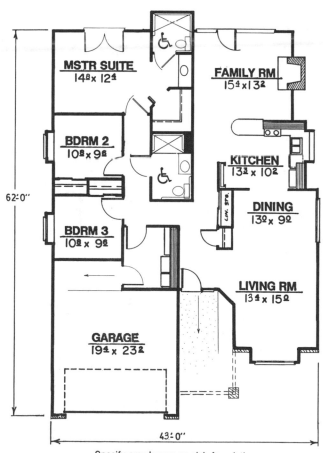

Specify crawlspace or slab foundation.

Total living area: 1,708 sq. ft.
(Not counting garage)

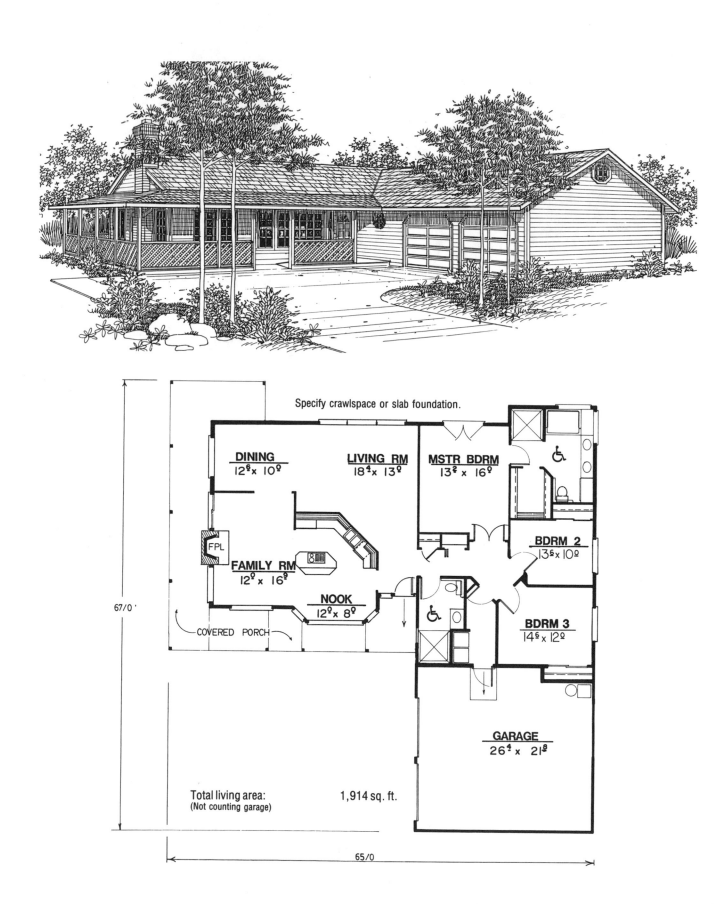

Specify crawlspace or slab foundation.

DINING
12⁶ x 10⁰

LIVING RM
18⁴ x 13⁰

MSTR BDRM
13² x 16⁰

FPL

FAMILY RM
12⁰ x 16⁹

NOOK
12⁰ x 8⁰

BDRM 2
13⁶ x 10⁰

BDRM 3
14⁶ x 12⁰

67/0'

COVERED PORCH

GARAGE
26⁴ x 21⁸

Total living area:
(Not counting garage)          1,914 sq. ft.

65/0

# INDEPENDENT LIVING CENTERS

## Alabama

Independent Living Center
3421 Fifth Avenue, South
Birmingham, AL 35222

## Alaska

Access Alaska
3550 Airport Way #3
Fairbanks, AK 99709

Alaska Division of Vocational Rehabilitation
Pouch F, M/S 0581
Juneau, AK 99811

Hope Cottages, Inc.
2805 Bering Street
Anchorage, AK 99503

## American Samoa

Samoa Center for IL
P.O. Box 3492
Pago Pago, AS 96799

## Arizona

Arizona Bridge ILC
1229 East Washington
Phoenix, AZ 85034

Community Outreach Program
268 West Adams Street
Tucson, AZ 85706

Disability Resource Center
1023 North Tyndall Avenue
Tucson, AZ 85719

Services to Advance IL
1700 First Avenue, Suite 114
Yuma, AZ 85364

## Arkansas

IL Services Center
5800 Asher Avenue
Little Rock, AR 72204

## California

Adult Independence Development
1190 Benton Street
Santa Clara, CA 95050

Brentwood Social Program
11301 Wilshire Blvd.
Los Angeles, CA 90073

C.A.P.H.-I.L.C.
1617 East Saginaw Way #109
Fresno, CA 93704

C.I.L. San Gabriel Valley
114 East Italia Street
Covina, CA 91723

Center for I.L.
2539 Telegraph Avenue
Berkeley, CA 94704

Center for I.L.
2231 East Garvey Avenue
West Covina, CA 91791

Comm. Rehab Services — ILC
4716 Brooklyn Avenue
Bldg. B, #15
Los Angeles, CA 90022

Community Resources
576 B Street, Suite 1
Santa Rosa, CA 95401

Community Resources — ILC
340 Soquel Avenue, Suite 115
Santa Cruz, CA 95062

Community Service Center
2864 University Avenue
San Diego, CA 92104

Darrell McDaniel I.L.C.
18 South Chester
Bakersfield, CA 93304

Darrell McDaniel I.L.C.
44815 Fig Avenue, Suite B
Lancaster, CA 93534

Darrell McDaniel I.L.C.
14354 Haynes Street
Van Nuys, CA 92401

Dayle McIntosh Center
150 W. Cerritos, Bldg. 4
Anaheim, CA 92805

Disabled Resources Center
1045 Pine Avenue
Long Beach, CA 90813

F.R.E.E.D.
154 Hughes Road #1
Grass Valley, CA 95945

Good Shepherd Center
4323 Leimert Blvd.
Los Angeles, CA 90008

Humboldt Access Project
712 Fourth Street
Eureka, CA 95501

I.L.C. of San Francisco
4429 Cabrillo Street
San Francisco, CA 94121

I.L. Resource Center
423 West Victoria
Santa Barbara, CA 93101

I.L. Skills Program
875 O'Neill Avenue
Belmont, CA 94002

Marin C.I.L.
710 4th Street
San Rafael, CA 94901

Northern California I.L.C.
555 Rio Lindo Avenue, Suite B
Chico, CA 95926

Resources for I.L.
1211 H Street #B
Sacramento, CA 95814

Rolling Start, Inc.
443 West 4th Street
San Bernardino, CA 92401

Southeast C.I.L.
12458 Rives Avenue
Downey, CA 90242

Westside C.I.L.
1516 Cravens Avenue
Torrance, CA 90501

Westside Center I.L.C.
12901 Venice Blvd.
Los Angeles, CA 90066

Winners Rehab & I.L.C.
15738 California Avenue
Paramount, CA 90723

## Colorado

Atlantis Community, Inc.
2937 East Galley Road
Colorado Springs, CO 80909

Atlantis Community, Inc.
4536 East Colfax
Denver, CO 80220

Atlantis Community, Inc.
2710 West Alameda Avenue
Denver, CO 80219

Center for I.L.
1245 East Colfax Avenue, Suite 219
Denver, CO 80218

Center for People with Disabilities
1450 15th Street
Boulder, CO 80302

Colorado Springs I.L.C.
122 South 16th Street
Colorado Springs, CO 80904

Greeley Resources
P.O. Box 5045
Greeley, CO 80631

Greeley Center
1734 8th Avenue
Greeley, CO 80631

Handicapped Information Center
424 Pine, Suite 101
Fort Collins, CO 80524

I.L.C.
835 Colorado Avenue
Grand Junction, CO 81501

Pueblo Goodwill Center
410 North Main
Pueblo, CO 81003

San Luis Valley Center
Box 990
Alamosa, CO 91101

## Connecticut

C.I.L. of Southwestern
959 Main Street
Stratford, CT 06497

Chaple Haven, Inc.
1040 Walley Avenue
New Haven, CT 06515

Independence Unlimited
410 Asylum Street
Hartford, CT 06103

## District of Columbia

D.C. Center for I.L.
1400 Florida Avenue, N.E., #3
Washington, DC 20002

I.L. for the Handicapped
1301 Belmont Street, N.W.
Washington, DC 20009

## Delaware

Easter Seal Center
240 North James Street, Suite 100
Wilmington, DE 19804

Independent Living, Inc.
159 Willis Road, #D
Dover, DE 19901

Independent Living, Inc.
818 South Broom Street
Wilmington, DE 19805

## Florida

C.I.L. in Central Florida
720 North Denning Drive
Winter Park, FL 32789

C.I.L. of North Florida, Inc.
1380 Ocala Road, #H4
Tallahassee, FL 32304

C.I.L. of Northwest Florida
3789 Nobles Street
Pensacola, FL 32514

Cathedral C.I.L.
3599 University Blvd. S.
Jacksonville, FL 32216

Center for Survival
1335 N.W. 14th Street
Miami, FL 33125

Florida Institute
307 East Seventh Street
Tallahassee, FL 32303

Self-Reliance, Inc.
12310 North Nebraska Avenue #5
Tampa, FL 33612

Space Coast Association
1127 South Patrick Drive #6
Satellite Beach, FL 32937

Space Coast Association
725 DeLeon Avenue, Suite 134
Titusville, FL 32780

## Georgia

Atlantic Center
1201 Glenwood Avenue, S.E.
Atlanta, GA 30316

I.L.C. Roosevelt Warm Springs
P.O. Box 1000
Warm Springs, GA 31830

Independent Living Program
212 West Oglethorpe
Albany, GA 31702

Independent Living Program
707 Pine Street
Macon, GA 31208

Independent Living Program
420 Mall Blvd.
Savannah, GA 31416

Independent Living Project
47 Trinity Avenue
Atlanta, GA 30334

## Hawaii

Big Island C.I.L.
205 Kinoole Street
Hilo, HI 96720

Hawaii C.I.L.
677 Ala Moana Blvd., #615
Honolulu, HI 96813

Kauai C.I.L.
P.O. Box 3529
Lihue, HI 96766

Maui C.I.L.
1446-D Lower Main Street, Room 105
Wailuku, HI 96793

## Iowa

Center for I.L. Rehab Services
524 4th Street
Des Moines, IA 50309

Hope Haven
1800 19th Street
Rock Valley, IA 51247

Independent Living Inc.
26 East Market
Iowa City, IA 52240

## Idaho

Center of Resources
707 North 7th, Suite A
P.O. Box 4185
Pocatello, ID 83201

Dawn Enterprises, Inc.
P.O. Box 388
Blackfoot, ID 83221

Housing Southwest #2
1102-4 West Finch Drive
Nampa, ID 83651

Idaho I.L. Services
650 West State Street
Boise, ID 83702

Stepping Stones, Inc.
124 East Third Street
Moscow, ID 83843

## Illinois

Access Living Metro Chicago
815 W. Van Buren Street, Suite 525
Chicago, IL 60607

ALMA
1642 North Winchester Avenue, Suite 100
Chicago, IL 60622

Center for Comprehensive Services
P.O. Box 2825
Carbondale, IL 62901

Center for Disabled Students
30 East Lake Street, Room 1045
Chicago, IL 60601

Central Illinois Center for Independent Living
222 North Western Avenue
Peoria, IL 61604

Fox River Valley Center
730-B West Chicago Street
Elgin, IL 60123

Illinois Department of Rehab Services
623 East Adams Street
Springfield, IL 62705

Illinois I.L.C.
710 East Ogden, Suite 207
Naperville, IL 60540

Impact C.I.L.
P.O. Box 338
Alton, IL 62002

Living Independence for Everyone
1544 East College Avenue
Normal, IL 61761

Northwestern Illinois C.I.L.
205 2nd Avenue
Sterling, IL 61081

P.A.C.E. Inc.
102 East Main Street, Suite 302
Urbana, IL 61801

R.A.M.P.
104 Chestnut Street
Rockford, IL 61101

Southern Illinois C.I.L.
780 East Grand Avenue
Carbondale, IL 62901

Springfield Center
426 West Jefferson
Springfield, IL 62702

West Cook C.I.L.
711 South 5th Avenue
Maywood, IL 60153

## Indiana

Center for I.L.
5800 Fairfield, Suite 210
Fort Wayne, IN 46807

Damar Homes, Inc.
6324 Kentucky Avenue
P.O. Box 41
Camby, IN 46113

## Kansas

Center for the Handicapped
1119 West 10th, Suite 2
Topeka, KS 66604

Cowley City Developmental Services
P.O. Box 133
Arkansas City, KS 67005

Independent Living of Southwestern Kansas
4808 West 9th
Wichita, KS 67212

Independence Inc.
1910 Haskell
Lawrence, KS 66046

Independent Connection
1710 West Schilling Road
Salina, KS 67401

Independent Living Program
2200 Gage Blvd.
VA Medical Center
Topeka, KS 66622

Link, Inc.
P.O. Box 1016
Hays, KS 67601

Network for the Disabled
313-A Broadway
P.O. Box 35
Valley Falls, KS 66088

Resource Center for I.L.
107 Barclay
Osage City, KS 66523

Three Rivers I.L.C.
810 4th Street
Wamego, KS 66547

## Kentucky

C.I.L. of Louisville
P.O. Box 35260
Louisville, KY 40232

Center for Accessible Living
835 West Jefferson, Suite 105
Louisville, KY 40204

Center for I.L.
1900 Brownsboro Road
Louisville, KY 40206

Contact, Inc.
212 West Broadway
Frankfort, KY 40601

West End Awareness
402 South 38th Street, #2C
Louisville, KY 40212

## Louisiana

Independent Living Center
320 North Carrolton Avenue, Suite 2C
New Orleans, LA 70119

New Horizons, Inc.
4030 Wallace Avenue
Shreveport, LA 71108

Southwest Louisiana I.L.C.
3104 Enterprise Blvd.
Lake Charles, LA 70601

Volunteers of America, I.L.C.
3131 1-10 Service Road N., #100
Metairie, LA 70002

## Massachusetts

AD-LIB
442 North Street
Pittsfield, MA 01201

ARC-I.L. Program
38 Hiramar Road
Hyannis, MA 02601

Boston Center
50 New Edgerly Road
Boston, MA 02115

Center for Living and Working, Inc.
600 Lincoln Street
Worcester, MA 01605

D.E.A.F., Inc.
215 Brighton Avenue
Allston, MA 02134

Independent Associates
693 Bedford Street
P.O. Box 146
Elmwood, MA 02337

Northeast I.L. Program
190 Hampshire Street, Suite 101B
Lawrence, MA 01840

Renaissance Program
21 Branch Street
Lowell, MA 01851

Stavros, Inc.
691 South East Street
Amherst, MA 01002

Student I.L. Experience
3 Randolph Street
Canton, MA 02021

Vision Foundation, Inc.
818 Mt. Auburn Street
Watertown, MA 02172

## Maryland

Maryland Citizens for Housing
6305-A Sherwood Road
Baltimore, MD 21239

## Maine

Alpha I — Maine I.L. Program
41 Acme Road
Brewer, ME 04412

Alpha I — Outreach Office
71 State Street
Augusta, ME 04330

Alpha I — Outreach Office
373 Main Street-Rear
Presque Isle, ME 04769

Independent Living Center
Bell Dorm, Husson College
Bangor, ME 04401

Maine I.L. Center
74 Winthrop Street
Augusta, ME 04330

Motivational Services, Inc.
114 State Street
Augusta, ME 04330

Shalom House, Inc.
90 High Street
Portland, ME 04101

The Together Place
150 Union Street
Bangor, ME 04401

## Michigan

Ann Arbor Center for I.L.
2568 Packard, Georgetown Mall
Ann Arbor, MI 48104

ARC/Ottowa County
1001 East Wesley
Muskegon, MI 49442

Center for Handicapped Affairs
918 Southland Street
Lansing, MI 48910

Center for I.L.
6044 Rochester Road
Troy, MI 48098

Community Living Center
935 Barlow
Traverse City, MI 49684

Cristo Rey Hispanic Center
1314 Ballard Street
Lansing, MI 48906

Family Resource Center
51 West Hancock
Detroit, MI 48201

Grand Rapids C.I.L.
3375 South Division
Grand Rapids, MI 49508

Independent Living
246 South River
Holland, MI 49423

Kalamazoo C.I.L.
833 West South
Kalamazoo, MI 49007

Midland I.L. Program
810 East Ashman
Midland, MI 48640

## Minnesota

C.I.L. of Northeastern Minnesota
2310 First Avenue
Hibbing, MN 55746

Options, Interstate Resource CIL
211 Demers Avenue
Holiday Mall
East Grand Forks, MN 56721

Accessible Space, Inc.
2550 University Avenue W., 301N
St. Paul, MN 55114

Homeowner Accessibility Loan Program
400 Sibley, #300
St. Paul, MN 55101

R.E.A.L.
317 West Main Street
Marshall, MN 52221

Vinland National Center
P.O. Box 308
Loretto, MN 55357

Rochester CIL
1306 7th Street NW
Rochester, MN 55901

## Mississippi

Alpha Home
P.O. Box 30
Hazlehurst, MS 39083

Independent Living Center
300 Capers Avenue
Jackson, MS 39203

## Missouri

Opportunities Unlimited
111 South 9th Street, Suite 211
Columbia, MO 65201

The Whole Person, Inc.
6301 Rockhill Road, Suite 30E
Kansas City, MO 64131

Rehabilitation Institute
3011 Baltimore
Kansas City, MO 64108

Independence Center
4380 West Pine Blvd.
St. Louis, MO 63108

Life Skill Foundation
609 North & South
St. Louis, MO 63130

Disabled Citizens Alliance
Box 675
Viburnum, MO 65566

## Montana

Montana Independent Living
1301 11th Avenue
Helena, MT 59601

Summit ILC
1280 South Third Street, West
Missoula, MT 59801

## Nebraska

Handicap Reach Out, Inc.
Box 948
345 W. Third Street
Chardon, NE 69337

League of Human Dignity
1423 O Street
Lincoln, NE 68508

## Nevada

Association for the Handicapped
P.O. Box 28458
Las Vegas, NV 89102

## New Jersey

Success Through IL Experiences
1501 Park Avenue
Asbury Park, NJ 07712

IL Resource Center
98 James Street, Suite 205
Edison, NJ 08820

Handicapped IL Program
44 Armory Street
Englewood, NJ 07631

## New Mexico

New Vistas ILC
500 Don Gaspar
Santa Fe, NM 87501

## New York

Options for Independence
55 Market Street
Auburn, NY 13021

Glens Falls ILC
P.O. Box 453
Glens Falls, NY 12801

Middletown CIL
208 Wickham Avenue
Middletown, NY 10940

Directions in IL
2636 West State Street, Suite A & B
Olean, NY 14760

Taconic Resources for Independence
89 Market Street
Poughkeepsie, NY 12601

Rockland ILC
235 North Main
Spring Valley, NY 10977

Troy Resource CIL
Troy Atrium, 4th & Broadway
Troy, NY 12180

Watertown ILC
Woolworth Building, Suite 500
Watertown, NY 13601

Capital District CIL
22 Colvin Avenue
Albany, NY 12206

IL for the Handicapped, Inc.
408 Jay Street, Room 401
Brooklyn, NY 11201

Buffalo IL Program
3108 Main Street
Buffalo, NY 14214

Suffolk City Handicapped Services
65 Jetson Lane
Central Islip, NY 11722

Western NY IL Program
2015 Transit
Elma, NY 14059

Long Island CIL/SUNY
Administration Bldg., #115
Farmingdale, NY 11735

Resource Center for Accessible Living, Inc.
602 Albany Avenue
Kingston, NY 12401

Services for the Physically Handicapped
240 Old Country Road, #610
Mineola, NY 11501

Visions
817 Broadway, 11th Floor
New York, NY 10003

Center for Independence of the Disabled in New York
853 Broadway, #611
New York, NY 10003

Rochester CIL
464 South Clinton Avenue
Rochester, NY 14620

Independent Living in the Capital District
2660 Albany Street
Schenectady, NY 12304

Arise CIL
501 East Fayette Street
Syracuse, NY 13202

Resource CIL
401 Columbia Street
Utica, NY 13502

Westchester County ILC
297 Knollwood Road
White Plains, NY 10607

Yonkers ILC
985 North Broadway
Yonkers, NY 10701

## North Carolina

Metrolina ILC
1012 S. Kings Drive
Doctor's Building G-2
Charlotte, NC 28283

## North Dakota

Housing Industry Training CIL
1007 NW 18th
Mandan, ND 58554

## Ohio

Total Living Concepts
7710 Reading Road, Suite 001
Cincinnati, OH 45237

Services for IL
25100 Euclid Avenue, Suite 105
Euclid, OH 44117

## Oklahoma

Green Country IL Resource Center
P.O. Box 2295
Bartlesville, OK 74005

Total Independent Living Today
601 North Porter
Norman, OK 73071

Ability Resources
1724 East 8th Street
Tulsa, OK 74104

## Oregon

Laurel Hill Center ILP
2621 Augusta Street
Eugene, OR 97403

Columbia Gorge Rehab Center
1306 Taylor Street
Hood River, OR 97031

Access Oregon
8213 SE 17th Avenue
Portland, OR 98202

## Pennsylvania

Resources for ILC
4721 Pine Street
Philadelphia, PA 19143

Allied Services for the Handicapped
475 Morgan Hwy.
Scranton, PA 18505

## Puerto Rico

Centro de Vida Independiente
Apartado 1681
Hato Rey, PR 00919

## Rhode Island

Pari Independent Living Center
Independence Square
500 Prospect Street
Pawtucket, RI 02860

Insight Independent Living
43 Jefferson Blvd.
Warwick, RI 02888

## South Carolina

SC VR ILP
1400 Boston Avenue
West Columbia, SC 29169

## South Dakota

Prairie Freedom Center for Disabled
Independence
800 West Avenue North
Sioux Falls, SD 57104

## Tennessee

Memphis CIL
163 North Angelus
Memphis, TN 38104

## Texas

Educational Support Services
P.O. Box 19028
U.T. at Arlington
Arlington, TX 76019

Texas Rehab Comm IL Services
118 E. Riverside Drive
Austin, TX 78704

Dallas Center for IL
8625 King George Drive, Suite 210
Dallas, TX 75235

Disabled Ability Resource Environment
8929 Viscount, Suite 101
El Paso, TX 79925

Houston Center for IL
3233 Wesleyan, Suite 102
Houston, TX 77027

Independent Life Styles
P.O. Box 742485
Houston, TX 77274

## U.S. Virgin Islands

Virgin Island Association for IL
P.O. Box 3305
Charlotte Amalie
St. Thomas, VI 00801

## Utah

Options for IL
47 North 200 East
Logan, UT 84321

## Vermont

Vermont CIL
174 River Street
Montpelier, VT 05602

## Virginia

Endependence Center of Northern Virginia
2111 Wilson Blvd., Suite 400
Arlington, VA 22201

Crossroads Center, Inc.
215 North Main Street
Bridgewater, VA 22812

Independence Resource Center
201 West Main Street, #8
Charlottesville, VA 22901

Woodrow Wilson CIL
Box 37, WWRC
Fishersville, VA 22939

Insight Enterprises
11832 Canon Blvd., Suite E
Newport News, VA 23606

Endependence Center, Inc.
100 W. Plume, Suite 224
Norfolk, VA 23510

Central Virginia ILC, Inc.
2900 West Broad Street
Richmond, VA 23230

IL Program VAMC Richmond
1201 Broad Rock Road
VAMC
Richmond, VA 23249

Shenandoah Valley ILC
21 South Kent Street
Winchester, VA 22601

## Washington

Vision and IL Services
119 N. Commercial, Suite 320
Bellingham, WA 98225

KITSAP Community Action Program
1200 Elizabeth Avenue
Bremerton, WA 98310

Independent Lifestyle Service
115 West Third
Ellensburg, WA 98926

Everett Coalition of People with Disabilities
1301 Hewett
Everett, WA 98201

Division of Vocational Rehabilitation IL
Services
P.O. Box 1788 M/A 21-C
Olympia, WA 98504

Center for Independence
407 14th Avenue, SE
Puyallup, WA 98371

Resource Center for the Handicapped
20150 45th Avenue, NE
Seattle, WA 98155

Vision Services
1401 Madison Street, Rm. 284
Seattle, WA 98104

Washington Coalition of Citizens with
Disabilities
3530 Stoneway N.
Seattle, WA 98103

Adventures — Independence Development
819 S. Hatch
Spokane, WA 98202

Spokane Coalition of People with Disabilities
107 W. Queen Avenue
Spokane, WA 99205

Coalition of Handicapped Organizations
6503-G East Mill Plain Blvd.
Vancouver, WA 98661

## West Virginia

Appalachian CIL
1427 Lee St., E.
Huntington, WV 25701

N. Central WV CIL
1000 Elmer W. Prince Drive
Morgantown, WV 26505

## Wisconsin

Curative Workshop, Inc.
1506 South Oneida Street
St. Elizabeth Hospital
Appleton, WI 54915

ILP Curative Rehab Center
2900 Curry Lane, Box 8027
Green Bay, WI 54308

Access to Independence
1954 East Washington Avenue
Madison, WI 53704

CIL
University of Wisconsin
Menomonie, WI 54751

Southeastern Wisconsin CIL
1545 S. Layton Blvd.
Milwaukee, WI 53215

IL Services
5000 W. National Avenue
Milwaukee, WI 53295

Society's Assets
720 High Street
Racine, WI 53402

Christian League for the Handicapped
P.O. Box 948
Walworth, WI 53184

## Wyoming

Wyoming IL Rehab
350 North Bighorn
Casper, WY 82601

Rehab Enterprises of Northeastern Wyoming
245 Broadway
Sheridan, WY 82801

# INFORMATION CENTERS

Accent on Information
P.O. Box 700
Bloomington, IL 61701
(309) 378-2961

Access/Abilities
P.O. Box 458
Mill Valley, CA 94942
(415) 388-3250

Assistive Device Center
California State University, Sacramento
6000 J Street
Sacramento, CA 95819
(916) 924-0280

Clearinghouse on the Handicapped
Office of Special Education & Rehabilitation
  Services
Department of Education
Switzer Building, Room 3119
Washington, DC 20202
(202) 732-1245

Council for Exceptional Children and Youth
1920 Association Drive
Reston, VA 22091
(703) 620-3660

Handicapped Education Exchange
11523 Charlton Drive
Silver Spring, MD 20902
(301) 681-7372

Information Center for Individuals with
  Disabilities, Inc.
20 Park Plaza
Boston, MA 02116
(617) 727-5540
(800) 462-5015

National Council of the Handicapped
800 Independence Avenue, S.W., Suite 814
Washington, DC 20591

National Information Center for Handicapped
  Children and Youth
P.O. Box 1492
Washington, DC 20013
(703) 522-0870

National Spinal Cord Hotline
National Study Center for Emergency Medical
  Systems
22 South Greene Street
Baltimore, MD 21201
(800) 526-3456 — National
(800) 638-1733 — Maryland

Rehabilitation International
25 East 21st Street
New York, NY 10010
(212) 420-1500

# ORGANIZATIONS

ABLEDATA
Adaptive Equipment Center
Newington Children's Hospital
181 East Cedar Street
Newington, CT 06111

American Amputee Foundation
P.O. Box 55218, Hillcrest Station
Little Rock, AR 72225
(501) 666-2523

American Council of the Blind
1010 Vermont Avenue, N.W., Suite 1100
Washington, DC 20005
(800) 424-8666
(202) 393-3666

American Foundation for the Blind
15 West 16th Street
New York, NY 10011
(212) 620-2000

American Paralysis Association
500 Morris Avenue
Springfield, NJ 07081
(201) 379-2000
(800) 225-0292

American Spinal Injury Association
250 E. Superior Street, Rm. 619
Chicago, IL 60611
(312) 908-3425

Amputees in Motion
P.O. Box 2703
Escondido, CA 92025
(619) 454-9300

Arthritis Society
250 Bloor Street E., Suite 401
Toronto, Ontario M4W 3P2

Association of the Deaf
271 Spadina Road, Suite 311
Toronto, Ontario M5R 2V3

Blind Organizations of Ontario with Self-Help
   Tactics (BOOST)
597 Parliament Street, Suite B3
Toronto, Ontario M4X 1W3

Canadian Association of Independent Living
   Centres
150 Kent Street, Suite 905
Ottawa, Ontario K1P 5P9

Canadian Rehabilitation Council for the
   Disabled
One Yonge Street, Suite 2110
Toronto, Ontario M5E 1E5

The Disabled Living Foundation
380-384 Harrow Road
London W9 2HU England

Disability Services
Boston University
Martin Luther King, Jr. Center
19 Deerfield Street
Boston, MA 02215

52 Association for the Handicapped, Inc.
441 Lexington Avenue
New York, NY 10007
(212) 986-5281

Fund for Equal Access to Society
1 Thomas Circle, N.W., Suite 350
Washington, DC 20005
(202) 223-0570

Handicaps Welfare Association
Whampoa Drive
(Behind Block 102)
Singapore 1232

Helen Keller National Center for Deaf-Blind
   Youths and Adults
111 Middle Neck Road
Sands Point, NY 11050

Independent Living Research Utilization
3400 Bissonnet, Suite 101
Houston, TX 77005
(713) 666-6244

International Polio Network
4502 Maryland Avenue
St. Louis, MO 63108
(314) 361-0475

International Social Service Canada
55 Parkdale Avenue
Ottawa, Ontario K1Y 1E5

Mobility International USA
P.O. Box 3551
Eugene, OR 97403
(503) 343-1284

Muscular Dystrophy Association, Inc.
810 Seventh Avenue
New York, NY 10019
(212) 586-0808

Muscular Dystrophy Association of Canada
150 Eglinton Avenue E., Suite 400
Toronto, Ontario M4P 1E8

National Amputation Foundation
1245 150th Street
Whitestone, NY 11357

National Association for the Visually
   Handicapped
22 W. 21 Street
New York, NY 10010
(212) 889-3141

National Association of the Physically
   Handicapped, Inc.
76 Elm Street
London, OH 43140

National Easter Seal Society
2023 West Ogden Avenue
Chicago, IL 60612
(312) 243-8400

National Federation of the Blind
1800 Johnson Street
Baltimore, MD 21230

National Handicap Housing Institute, Inc.
4556 Lake Drive
Robbinsdale, MN 55422
(612) 535-9771

National Information Center for Handicapped
   Children and Youth
P.O. Box 1492
Washington, DC 20013
(703) 522-3332

National Multiple Sclerosis Society
205 East 42nd Street
New York, NY 10017

National Rehabilitation Information Center
8455 Colesville Road, Suite 935
Silver Spring, MD 20910-3319
(800) 346-2742
(301) 588-9284

National Stroke Association
300 E. Hampden Avenue, Suite 240
Englewood, CO 80110-2622
(303) 762-9922

People United for Self-Help in Ontario (PUSH)
597 Parliament Street, Suite 204
Toronto, Ontario M4X 1W3

Promote Real Independence for the Disabled
and Elderly (PRIDE)
71 Plaza Court
Groton, CT 06340

Rehabilitation International
25 East 21st Street
New York, NY 10010
(212) 420-1500

The Royal Association for Disability and
Rehabilitation
25 Mortimer Street
London W1 N8A England

Self-Help Clearinghouse of Metropolitan
Toronto
40 Orchard View Blvd., Suite 215
Toronto, Ontario M4R 1B9

Spina Bifida and Hydrocephalus Association of
Canada
Toronto Chapter
61 Stonedene Blvd.
Willowdale, Ontario M2R 3C8

Spina Bifida Association of America
1700 Rockville Pike, Suite 540
Rockville, MD 20852
(800) 621-3141

Stroke Recovery Association
170 The Donway W., Suite 122
Don Mills, Ontario M3C 2G3

Technical Aids and Assistance for the Disabled
1950 West Roosevelt Road
Chicago, IL 60608
(800) 346-2939
(312) 421-3373

United Cerebral Palsy Associations, Inc.
66 E. 34th Street
New York, NY 10016

World Institute on Disability
1720 Oregon Street, Suite 4
Berkeley, CA 94703
(415) 486-8314

# AMPUTEE SUPPORT GROUPS

## National

American Amputee Foundation National
Headquarters
P.O. Box 55218
Little Rock, AR 72225

Amputees in Motion, International
475 Marview Drive
Solana Beach, CA 92075

Federation of the Handicapped
211 W. 14th Street
New York, NY 10011

52 Association for the Handicapped
441 Lexington Avenue, Suite 502
New York, NY 10017

National Amputee Foundation
1245 150th Street
Whitestone, NY 11357

National Organization on Disability
910 16th Street, N.W.
Washington, DC 20006

## California

Amputees Are Able
1632 Garden
San Bernardino, CA 92404

Amputees Caring Together
197 Arneill Road
Camarillo, CA 90310

Direct Link
P.O. Box 6762
Santa Barbara, CA 92075

Direct Link
222422 W. Alamota
Saugus, CA 93160

Mutual Amputee Aid Foundation
P.O. Box 1200
Lomita, CA 90717

## Colorado

Gil Gillespie
Plaza Wood Creek/ Box 5159
Mt. Crested Butte, CO 81225

## District of Columbia

Mary Lilla Browne
P.O. Box 18259
Washington, DC 20036

## Florida

Dr. John Bowker
630 Solana Prodo
Coral Gables, FL 33156

Amputee Discussion Group
Baptist Hospital
8900 N. Kendall Drive
Miami, FL 33137

Florida Amputee Hotline
P.O. Box 370788
Miami, FL 33137

Amputee Support Group
Bon Secours Hospital
1050 N.E. 125th
North Miami, FL 33161

Central Florida Amputee Service Group
P.O. Box 561142
Orlando, FL 32856-1142

A.F.T.E.R. Inc. — Amputees for Training,
Education and Rehab
8408 W. McNab Road
Tamarac, FL 33321

C.A.L.D. — Children Afflicted with Limb
Deficiencies
9127 New Orleans Drive
Orlando, FL 32818

Pen-Parent Education Network of Florida
2215 East Henry Avenue
Tampa, FL 33610

## Iowa

Robin Smith
408 S. Dodge
Iowa City, IA 52240

## Illinois

Donna Boddy
8826 Butterfield Lane
Orland Park, IL 60642

Amputee Service Association
P.O. Box A 3819
Chicago, IL 60690

Families and Amputees in Motion
10046 S. Western Avenue, Suite 10
Chicago, IL 60643

## Indiana

Michiana Amputee Support Group
3449 S. High
South Bend, IN 46614

## Kansas

L.E.A.P.S. Across the Heartland (Lower
Extremity Amputees Providing Support)
P.O. Box 7906
Shawnee Mission, KS 66207

## Louisiana

Trisha Cook
10105 Idlewood Place
River Ridge, LA 70123

## Massachusetts

Commonwealth of Massachusetts
2513 8th Street
Charlestown, MA 02129

Helping Hands
P.O. Box 2348
Farmington, MA 01701

## Maryland

Amputee Association of Maryland
c/o Kernan Hospital
2200 Forest Park Avenue
Baltimore, MD 21207

## Michigan

A.L.A.R.M. — Amputee of Legs of Arms
Resource Meetings
1301 North Main Street
Adrian, MI 49221

Amputee Support and Service Group
31917 Wayburn Drive
Farmington Hills, MI 48018

APPENDIX: AMPUTEE SUPPORT GROUPS ■ 153

Michigan Amputee Foundation, Inc.
6849 S. Division Avenue
Grand Rapids, MI 49508

## Mississippi

Mississippi Amputee Support Group
4901 McWillie Circle
Jackson, MS 39206

## Missouri

Suzanne King & Dave Farris
c/o St. Joe YMCA
315 S. 6th Street
St. Joseph, MO 64501

Amputees in Motion
P.O. Box 335
Columbia, MO 65205

Maureen Raffensperger, R.P.T.
Heartland Centre
Physical Therapy Dept.
701 Faraon Street
St. Joseph, MO 64501

## Nebraska

Hotline for the Handicapped
P.O. Box 94987
301 Centennial Mall S.
Lincoln, NE 68509

## New Jersey

Elaine Naismith
7 Barberry Way
Essex Fells, NJ 07021

PACT — Parents of Amputee Children
Together
c/o Kessler Institute for Rehabilitation
Pleasant Valley Way
West Orange, NJ 07052

In-Step
Englewood Hospital
350 Engle Street
Englewood, NJ 07631

S.H.A.G. Self-Help Amputee Group
c/o Kessler Institute
Pleasant Valley Way
West Orange, NJ 07052

## Nevada

Northern Nevada Amputee Support Group
710 Marion Way
Sparks, NV 89431

## New York

Thelma W. Ryan
19 Pine Tree Lane
Levittown, NY 11756

Michael Madden
242 Bloomingrove Drive
Troy, NY 12180

Amputee Support Network
Box 2501
Liverpool, NY 13090

Staten Island Amputee Club
475 Seaview Avenue
Staten Island, NY 10305

## Ohio

Amputee Support Group
222 Pleasanthill Court
Centerville, OH 45459

Central Ohio Amputee Support Group
P.O. Box 1701
Columbus, OH 43216

I CAN
2380 Overlook Road
Cleveland Heights, OH 44118

## Oklahoma

Preston Cross
3384 Del Aire Place
Del City, OK 73115

## Oregon

Jan Morrissey
4135 North Court Avenue
Portland, OR 97217

## Pennsylvania

AMP-PEER
Magee Rehab Hospital
1600 Arch Street
Philadelphia, PA 19102

Amputee Support Group
Harmarville Rehab Center
P.O. Box 11460
Guys Run Road
Pittsburgh, PA 15238

Amputee Support Group of Altoona
c/o Mercy Hospital
2500 7th Avenue
Altoona, PA 16603

Amputee Support Group
Rehab Hospital of York
1850 Normandie Drive
York, PA 17404

Amputees & Non-Functional Limbs Support
Group
c/o Altoona Rehab Hospital
2005 Valley View Blvd.
Altoona, PA 16602

Community Amputee Support Team
P.O. Box 400, R.D. 6
Coatsville, PA 19320

Community Amputee Support Team
Bryn Mawr Rehab Hospital
414 Paoli Pike
Malvern, PA 19355

Community Amputee Support Team
503 N. Water Street
Lititz, PA 17543

## Tennessee

Barbara Lear
447 E. Market Street
Kingsport, TN 37660

Sheryl Jackson, R.N., C.N.S.
D-2120, M.C.N.
Nashville, TN 37232

## Texas

East Texas Amputee Foundation
915 Old Hickory Road
Tyler, TX 75703

Hill Country Amputee Foundation
P.O. Box 706
Kerrville, TX 78028

North Texas Amputee Support Group
5427 Redfield
Dallas, TX 75235

Pilot Parents Training Program
1704 Seamist, Suite 450
Houston, TX 77008

S.O.A.R., Inc. — Stepping Out and Reaching
3050 Post Oak Blvd.
Houston, TX 77056

Texamo Health Care Center
120 S. Crockett
Sherman, TX 75090

West Texas Amputee Foundation
3521-A 34th Street
Lubbock, TX 79404

**Virginia**

Bill Haneke
P.O. Box 11192
Richmond, VA 23230

# PRODUCTS

## Household Products

### Honeywell Lo-Vision Thermostat
Enlarged raised numbers indicate temperature range for quick recognition by sight or touch. A click can be heard, and an indent is felt for every two degrees of dial movement. The thermostat includes an enlarged temperature dial and indicator. Designed to replace virtually all 24-volt thermostats. Comes with complete instructions, large print Users Hang Tag, and Braille card. Priced well under $50.

Available from:
American Foundation for the Blind
Consumer Products
15 West 16th Street
New York, NY 10011
(212) 620-2000

### Contour Tap Turner
This is a multi-purpose tool for turning taps, knobs, keys, etc. When pressed against an object, the spring-loaded metal pins help provide an improved grip. Priced around $15.

Available from:
Cleo Inc.
3957 Mayfield Road
Cleveland, OH 44121
(800) 321-0595

### Maddatap
This device permits the intermittent use of water from a standard tap without shutting off or turning on valves each time. It screws onto the end of the faucet. The water is then turned on but will not run out until the slim plastic rod hanging down from the spout is pushed. A container or hand can be pressed against the rod and water will stay on until pressure is released.

Available from:
Maddak Inc.
Pequannock, NJ 07440-1993
(800) 443-4926
(201) 694-0500

### Leveron®
This door lever is easily installed and requires less than one-third the force of metal lever hardware to operate. Priced under $15.

Available from:
Lindustries, Inc.
21 Shady Hill Road
Weston, MA 02193
(617) 237-8177, 235-5452

### Portable Door Knob Turner
The user can carry this portable door knob turner anywhere. Made of one-piece molded plastic, it increases leverage when turning rotating knobs. A hook-like end works on pull-type handles and car doors. Priced under $15.

Available from:
Access to Recreation, Inc.
2509 E. Thousand Oaks Blvd., Suite 430
Thousand Oaks, CA 91362
(800) 634-4351

### Automatic Door Opener
Power Access automatic door opener accommodates a number of door sizes, opening forces, and operating times. The unit plugs into a standard 110-volt wall outlet.

Available from:
Power Access Corporation
Bridge Street
P.O. Box 235
Collinsville, CT 06022
(800) 344-0088
(203) 693-0751

## Automatic Sliding Door Operator

Horton offers an automatic sliding door operator that can be installed on existing doors as well as new construction. It operates with a push button or remote switching. Horton also offers a manual/automatic swing door operator (Easy Access™) which can be installed on existing swing doors.

Available from:
Horton Automatics, A Division of the Dallas Corporation
4242 Baldwin Blvd.
Corpus Christi, TX 78405
(800) 531-3111
(512) 888-5591

## Miscellaneous Items

Independent Living Aids, Inc. offers a large range of household items including a milk carton holder, bottle grip, door knob opener, and pickup tool. Most are priced under $5 with some around $1.

Available from:
Independent Living Aids, Inc.
27 East Mall
Plainview, NY 11803
(800) 537-2118

## Communication Systems

### Door Scope

This door scope offers a 2-inch diameter viewing area and allows visitors to be identified even if they are standing 6 to 7 feet from the door. It has a wide angle view, allowing the user to stand a distance from the door and still see clearly. Priced around $40.

Available from:
LS&S Group, Inc.
P.O. Box 673
1808-G Janke Drive
Northbrook, IL 60065
(800) 468-4789

### Signal Systems for Hearing-Impaired

NFSS Inc. offers products for the hearing-impaired including doorbell, telephone, and baby cry signalers, alarm clocks, pagers, smoke detectors, answering machines, and other accessories.

Available from:
NFSS, Inc.
8120 Fenton Street
Silver Spring, MD 20910
(301) 589-6670/TDD
(301) 589-6671/Voice

### Tactile Communicator

Sonic Alert Tactile Communicator is a wireless radio and paging system for deaf-blind communications. It was designed by the Research Department of the Helen Keller National Center.

Available from:
Sonic Alert
1750 West Hamlin Road
Rochester Hills, MI 48309
(313) 656-3110

### Speak-A-Lock

Allows user to answer the door without moving from the bed or chair, talking to the person at the door and then unlocking the door as needed. Used with existing keys and locks.

Available from:
Newton Wheelchairs U.S.A.
21209 Lago Circle, 12E
Boca Raton, FL 33433
(407) 483-7184

## Environmental Controls

### Encoscan, Kincontrol
TASH Inc. offers several environmental control units. The Encoscan can serve as a five-function scanner and controller or can be set up to control many additional functions. It has a built-in ultrasonic receiver for remote operation and can be used for placing and receiving phone calls, unlocking doors, controlling TVs, operating call bells, etc. Priced around $1500. The Kincontrol, priced at around $800, allows control of up to ten functions, and accessories are available. Single function environmental units are also available.

Available from:
TASH Inc.
Technical Aids & Systems for the Handicapped
  Inc.
70 Gibson Drive, Unit 12
Markham, Ontario L3R 4C2
(416) 475-2212

### Control Systems
Du-It offers several environmental control systems designed to control appliances, telephones, lighting, etc. Operated by remote control, they range in price from under $500 to about $1500.

Available from:
Du-It Control Systems Group
8765 Twp Road 513
Shreve, OH 44676
(216) 567-2906

### Ezra System
Ezra is a single-switch environmental control system that functions through a menu appearing on a television screen. It can be programmed to control a number of functions. The base unit is priced under $1000.

Available from:
Access to Recreation, Inc.
2509 E. Thousand Oaks Blvd., Suite 430
Thousand Oaks, CA 91362
(800) 634-4351

### X-10 Powerhouse
This is a home control system allowing the user to remotely control a number of modules inside or outside the home. Priced from $25.

Available from:
X-10 (USA) Inc.
185A LeGrand Avenue 1200
Northvale, NJ 07647
(800) 526-0027
(201) 784-9700

X-10 Home Controls Inc.
Aerowood Drive, Unit 20
Mississauga, Ontario L4W 2S7
(800) 387-3346
(416) 624-4446

### Control Devices
The Scanning X-10 Powerhouse controls up to sixteen appliances and/or lights. Control 1 is an environmental control designed to respond to computer-type commands (though it can be operated without a computer).

Available from:
Prentke Romich Company
1022 Heyl Road
Wooster, OH 44691
(800) 642-8255
(216) 262-1984

## Bathing Equipment

### Eaton E-Z Bath
The E-Z Bath is made of sturdy, non-corrosive aluminum and is easy to install and use. A seat extends to wheelchair height and can be raised

or lowered into and out of the tub. No plumbing or electrical work is required. Priced around $600.

Available from:
Eaton E-Z Bath Co.
P.O. Box 712
Garden City, KS 67846

### One-Piece Shower and Tub/Shower Modules

Fiat Products offers several models of one-piece acrylic shower and tub/shower modules. Grab bars are located in the proper positions. Some units have molded seats; others have fold-up teakwood seats. All have anti-skid floors.

Available from:
Fiat Products
1 Michael Court
Plainview, NY 11803
(516) 349-7000

### Bathroom Safety Rail and Shower Seat

The Tub Guard™ Bathroom Safety Rail mounts securely on the tub without using tools. It is priced under $60. Ergonomically designed, it has a textured surface for a comfortable, safe grip. The Ashbourne Shower Seat has a height-adjustable seat, armrests, and requires no tools to assemble. Priced under $175.

Available from:
Access to Recreation, Inc.
2509 E. Thousand Oaks Blvd.
Suite 430
Thousand Oaks, CA 91362
(800) 634-4351

### Minor-Aquatec Bath Lift

This bath lift is hydraulically operated and can be installed in any standard bathtub. It acts as a transfer bench and lowers the bather into the water.

Available from:

Aquatec
Health Care Products, Incorporated
Allegheny Station P.O. Box 7066
Pittsburgh, PA 15212

### Tri-Grip Rail

This security rail for the bathtub offers three gripping heights. Clamps fit all modern bathtubs.

Available from:
Frohock-Stewart, Inc.
Bath Patient Aid Products and Bath Accessories
455 Whitney Avenue
P.O. Box 330
Northboro, MA 01532-0330
(800) 343-6059
(617) 393-2543 in Massachusetts

### Bathing and Transfer Systems

Silcraft Corporation offers a complete line of bathing and transfer systems. "Bather 2001" is for sit-down bathing and showering. "Traverse" is a mobile power lift. "Easy Access Shower Systems" have no threshold and provide easy entry for shower chairs.

Available from:
The Silcraft Corporation
528 Hughes Drive
Traverse City, MI 49684
(800) 678-7100
(616) 946-4221

### Bath Aids

Guardian Products offers transfer benches and shower chairs, some with height adjustment, as well as grab bars (permanent and movable).

Available from:
Guardian® Products, Inc.
Sunrise Medical
12800 Wentworth Street
Box C-4522
Arleta, CA 91331-4522
(818) 504-2820

### Jacuzzi

The Jacuzzi Whirlpool Bath creates a consistent air/water mixture that results in a soothing massage. Air jets can be individually adjusted.

Available from:
Jacuzzi Whirlpool Bath
100 N. Wiget Lane
Walnut Creek, CA 94598
(415) 938-7070

## Lifting Aids

### Silver-Glide® Stairway Lift

This stairway lift can be installed on either side of a stairway, has an extra-wide seat, and the seat and footrest fold up when not in use. Adaptive Products also offers several other models of stairway lift, including one with a custom-made track for curved configurations.

Available from:
Adaptive Products Incorporated
645 S. Addison Road
Addison, IL 60101
(708) 832-0203

Lifting aids — stair lifts, wheelchair lifts, etc. — are available from:
Garaventa (Canada) Ltd.
P.O. Box L-1
Blaine, WA 98230

Garaventa (Canada) Ltd.
7505 134A Street
Surrey, B.C. V3W 7B3
(800) 663-6556
(604) 594-0422

Handi-Lift, Inc.
436 West Main Street
Wyckoff, NJ 07481
(800) 432-LIFT
(201) 891-8097

Cheney
2445 South Calhoun Road
P.O. Box 188
New Berlin, WI 53151
(800) 782-1222
(414) 782-1100

Florlift of New Jersey, Inc.
41 Lawrence Street
East Orange, NJ 07017
(201) 429-2200

NWC
The National Wheel-O-Vator Company, Inc.
P.O. Box 1308
Patterson, LA 70392
(800) 551-9095

## Ramps

Ramps are available from:
JH Industries
8901 E. Pleasant Valley Road
Independence, OH 44131
(800) 321-4968, (216) 524-7520

## Other

### Independent Living Home Appraisal

Consumer Care™ offers an Independent Living Home Appraisal Questionnaire/Checklist. It is designed for those persons faced with adapting housing to provide a safe, efficient, comfortable living environment for a disabled person. The Questionnaire/Checklist covers more than 200 criteria, based on the current literature, which influence the disabled person's level of independence. Priced at around $15. A Follow-up Assessment of particular, individual needs is available for under $100.

Available from:
Consumer Care™
P.O. Box 684
810 N. Water Street
Sheboygan, WI 53082-0684
(414) 459-8353

# BOOKS AND PUBLICATIONS

*Access to Housing in the '80s: Strategies and Case Studies for Adaptable and Accessible Housing.* $10.

Available from:
Association of Bay Area Governments
Metrocenter
8th and Oak Streets
Oakland, CA 94604
(415) 464-7900

✱✱✱

*The Accessible Bathroom*
Discusses accessible design with illustrations, detailed dimensions, and construction tips. Includes discussion of modifying existing equipment. Written by the Design Coalition, Inc., Madison, Wisconsin's community design and planning center. $8.50.

*An Accessible Entrance: Ramps.* $7.50.

Available from:
Access to Independence Inc.
1954 East Washington Avenue
Madison, WI 53704
(608) 251-7575

✱✱✱

*Adaptable Dwellings*

Available from:
HUD User
P.O. Box 280
Germantown, MD 20874

✱✱✱

*Aging and Developmental Disabilities: Issues and Approaches*, edited by Matthew P. Janicki and Henryk M. Wisniewski

Available from:

Paul H. Brookes Publishing Company
P.O. Box 10624
Baltimore, MD 21285-0624

✱✱✱

*Aging with a Disability*, by Roberta B. Trieschmann, Ph.D.

*Our Aging Parents: A Practical Guide to Eldercare*, by Colette Browne and Roberta Onzuka-Anderson

Available from:
Demos Publications, Inc.
156 Fifth Avenue, Suite 1018
New York, NY 10010

✱✱✱

*Coping with Disability*, by Peggy Jay
Includes advice on making life easier in the home and managing independent living at home.

*Design Data for Wheelchair Children*, by Brian C. Goldsmith
Intended for architects and other professionals involved in designing environments for the handicapped child, specifically children in wheelchairs.

*The Directory for Disabled People*, 5th edition, compiled by Ann Darnborough and Derek Kinrade

Available from:
The Royal Association for Disability & Rehabilitation
25 Mortimer Street
London W1N 8AB England

✱✱✱

*Disabled Policy: America's Programs for the Handicapped*, by Edward Berkowitz
Discusses many American governmental policies

toward civil rights and independent living programs as well as workers' compensation, social security disability insurance, and vocational rehabilitation. $24.95.

Available from:
Cambridge University Press
32 E. 57th Street
New York, NY 10022

\* \* \*

"The Do-able Renewable Home" (brochure)

Available from:
AARP
Fulfillment, D 12470
1909 K Street, NW
Washington, DC 20049

\* \* \*

*Elderly Housing Options*, by Terrence J. Scott and Robert F. Maziarka. $40.

Available from:
Pluribus Press Inc.
160 E. Illinois Street
Chicago, IL 60611
(312) 467-0424

\* \* \*

*Handicapped at Home*, by Sydney Foot, published by Croom Helm
This book's aim is to encourage the handicapped person to live as full a life as possible.

*Housing for Older Adults: Options and Answers*, editors Robert L. Cosby and Terri Flynn. $10.

Available from:
The National Council on the Aging
600 Maryland Avenue S.W.
Washington, DC 20024
(202) 479-1200

\* \* \*

*Home Management, Housing and Furniture*, and others in the *Equipment for the Disabled* series
*Equipment for the Disabled* is a series of handbooks on disability equipment and products designed to maximize capabilities. Includes information on manufacturers and distributors. Illustrated.

Available from:
Equipment for the Disabled
Mary Marlborough Lodge
Nuffield Orthopaedic Centre
Headington
Oxford OX3 7LD England

\* \* \*

*Home Safety Guide for Older People*, by Jon Pynoos and Evelyn Gohen
A guide to making living at home safer and easier for the aging. Identifies problems and hazards, offers remedies, and directs the reader to supply sources.

Available from:
Serif Press
1331 H Street N.W.
Washington, DC 20005

\* \* \*

*Housing Adaptability Guidelines: A Concept to Make All Housing Accessible*

Available from:
State of California
Department of Rehabilitation
Topanga, CA 90290

\* \* \*

*Housing and Support Services for Physically Disabled Persons in Canada*

Available from:
Canadian Rehab. Council for the Disabled
One Yonge Street, Suite 2110
Toronto, Ontario M5E 1E5

\* \* \*

*Housing for the Elderly*, by Masoud Rabizadeh. $5.

Available from:
University of Oregon, University Publications
101 Chapman Hall
Eugene, OR 97403
(503) 686-5396

*Housing for the Elderly: Options and Design.*
$59.50

Available from:
Nichols Publishing
11 Harts Lane, Suite 1
East Brunswick, NJ 08816
(201) 238-4880

✳✳✳

*Housing for the Handicapped and Disabled: A Guide for Local Action*, by Marie M. Thompson.
$7. Available from:
National Association of Housing and
Redevelopment Officials
1320 18th Street, NW
Washington, DC 20036
(202) 429-2960

✳✳✳

*Housing Interiors for the Disabled and Elderly*, by Bettyann B. Raschko. $51.95.

Available from:
Van Nostrand Reinhold
115 Fifth Avenue
New York, NY 10003
(212) 254-3232

✳✳✳

*Housing Needs and the Elderly*, by Edgar A. Rose. $41.95.

Available from:
Gower Publishing Co.
Old Post Road
Brookfield, VT 05036
(802) 276-3162

✳✳✳

*How to Create Interiors for the Disabled: A Guidebook for Family and Friends*, by Jane Randolph Cary
Emphasizing basic remodeling techniques, the book is designed to help the reader create practical, realistic, attractive living environments.

Available from:
Pantheon Books, Inc.
Division of Random House, Inc.

201 E. 50th Street
New York, NY 10022
(800) 638-6460

✳✳✳

*Ideas for Making Your Home Accessible*
Tips and ideas (many illustrated) for building and remodeling. $6.50.

Available from:
Accent on Living
P.O. Box 700
Bloomington, IL 61702-9956

✳✳✳

*Kitchen Sense for Disabled People*, edited by Gwen Conacher, published by Croom Helm for the DLF
Gives practical, detailed advice on planning and equipping a kitchen, aids to make life easier for the handicapped person.

*Handling the Young Cerebral Palsied Child at Home*, by Nancie R. Finnie, published by William Heinemann Medical Books.

Available from:
Haigh & Hochland Ltd.
International University Booksellers
The Precinct Centre
Oxford Road
Manchester M13 9QA England

✳✳✳

*Old Homes, New Families: Innovative Living Arrangements for Older Persons*, by Gordon Streib. $40.

Available from:
Columbia University Press
562 W. 113th Street
New York, NY 10025
(212) 316-7100

✳✳✳

*Physical Management for the Quadriplegic Patient*, 2nd edition, by Jack R. Ford and Bridget Duckworth
Covers the full scope of the topic including a complete chapter on household management and

an appendix with house design plans. $59.

Available from:
F.A. Davis Company
1915 Arch Street
Philadelphia, PA 19103-9954
(800) 523-4049

✴✴✴

*Planning, Creating and Financing Housing for Handicapped People*, by Roberta Nelson-Walker

*Wheelchair to Independence: Architectural Barriers Eliminated*, by Ernest M. Gutman with Carolyn R. Gutman

Available from:
Charles C. Thomas
2600 S. First Street
Springfield, IL 62794
(217) 789-8980

✴✴✴

*Seniors Housing: A Development and Management Handbook.* $40.

Available from:
National Association of Home Builders
15 and M Streets, NW
Washington, DC 20005
(800) 368-5242 ext. 463

✴✴✴

*Spinal Network — The Total Resource for the Wheelchair Community*, by Sam Maddox

Covers all aspects of information on spinal cord injury. Softcover $26.95, spiral-bound $27.95.

*From Toys to Computers: Access for the Physically Disabled Child*

Available from:
Access to Recreation, Inc.
2509 E. Thousand Oaks Blvd., Suite 430
Thousand Oaks, CA 91362

✴✴✴

*The Wheelchair Child*, by Philippa Russell
A handbook for parents of the child confined to a wheelchair.

Available from:
Souvenir Press Ltd.
43 Great Russell Street
London WC1B 3PA, England

✴✴✴

*Where Will You Live Tomorrow?: The Complete Guide to Planning for Your Retirement Housing*, by Michael Sumichrast, Ronald Shafer, and Marika Sumichrast
Discusses major issues of housing costs, design, and planning.

Available from:
Dow Jones-Irwin
1818 Ridge Road
Homewood, IL 60430
(800) 634-3961

# MAGAZINES AND NEWSLETTERS

*Ability*
P.O. Box 370788
Miami, FL 33137
(305) 751-2525

*Accent on Living Magazine*
Gillun Road and High Drive
P.O. Box 700
Bloomington, IL 61701
(309) 378-2961

*Achievement*
925 N.W. 122nd
North Miami, FL 33161

*Advocate*, New York State Newsletter for the
Disabled
Office of Advocate for the Disabled
One Empire State Plaza
Albany, NY 12223-0001

*Ageing International*
International Federation on Ageing
1909 K Street, N.W.
Washington, DC 20049

*Breakout*
400 E. Randolph, Suite 223
Chicago, IL 60601

*Bulletins on Science and Technology for the
Handicapped*
Amer. Assoc. for the Advancement of Science
Office of Opportunities in Science
1776 Massachusetts Avenue, N.W.
Washington, DC 20036

*Can-Do*
5427 Redfield
Dallas, TX 75235

*Challenged American*
Box 4310
Sunland, CA 91040
(818) 353-3380

*Disabled USA*
1111 20th Street, N.W.
Washington, DC 20036

*Handicap News*
3060 East Bridge Street, #342
Brighton, CO 80601

*Handicapped Americans Reports*
951 Pershing Drive
Silver Spring, MD 20910

*ILRU Insights*
The National Newsletter for Independent Living
Independent Living Research Utilization
3400 Bissonnet, Suite 101
Houston, TX 77005
(713) 666-6244

*In-Step Newsletter*
350 Engle Street
Englewood, NJ 07631

*Mainstream*
861 Sixth Avenue, Suite 610
San Diego, CA 92101

*Mental and Physical Disability Law Reporter*
American Bar Association Commission on the
Mentally Disabled
1800 M Street, N.W.
Washington, DC 20036

*NCILP Newsletter*
National Council of Independent Living
Programs
4397 Laclede Avenue
St. Louis, MO 63120

*National Information Center for Handicapped
Children and Youth Newsletter*
P.O. Box 1492
Washington, DC 20013

*Paraplegia Life*
National Spinal Cord Injury Association
149 California Street
Newton, MA 02158

*Paraplegia News*
5201 N. 19th Avenue, Suite 111
Phoenix, AZ 85015

*Programs for the Handicapped — Clearinghouse
on the Handicapped*
Office of Sp. Ed. and Rehabilitation Services
U.S. Dept. of Education
Room 3119, Switzer Bldg.
Washington, DC 20202

*Project Newsletter*
SUNY/Buffalo
3435 Main Street
517 Kimball Tower
Buffalo, NY 14214

*SIA Newsletter*
Spinal Injuries Association
Yeoman House
76 St. James's Lane
London N10 3DF England

*Voice of the Physically Challenged*
L.I. Family Publications
222 Sunrise Highway
Rockville Center
New York, NY 11570

*Whole Access Quarterly*
SR 12479, Box 209
Phoenicia, NY 12464

# CATALOGS

Access to Recreation, Inc.
2509 E. Thousand Oaks Blvd., Suite 430
Thousand Oaks, CA 91362
Home gym, exercise and recreation equipment.
Ezra environmental control system. Reachers,
dressing aids, tub rail, shower seat, canes and
walkers, wheelchair accessories, exercise and
therapy aids, writing and office aids, household
and kitchen items. Books and videos.

Adaptive Products Incorporated
645 S. Addison Road
Addison, IL 60101
(708) 832-0203
Stairway lifts, wheelchair lifts, porch lifts.

AliMed
297 High Street
Dedham, MA 02026-9135
(617) 329-2900 (information number)
Wheelchair and walker accessories, household
items, bath and shower aids. Products must be
ordered through a physician.

Aqua Glass Corporation
P.O. Box 412
Industrial Park
Adamsville, TN 38310
(901) 632-0911
Showers for adaptable housing.

Consumer Care™
810 N. Water Street
P.O. Box 684
Sheboygan, WI 53082-0684
Wheelchair accessories, positioning aids, other
equipment.

Du-It Control Systems Group
8765 Twp Rd. 513
Shreve, OH 44676-9421
(216) 567-2906
Wheelchair control systems, environmental
control systems.

Dwyer Products Corporation
418 N. Calumet Avenue
Michigan City, IN 46360
(800) 348-8508
Adjustable kitchen cabinets and counters.

Fleetwood
P.O. Box 1259
Holland, MI 49422-1259
(616) 396-1142
Mainly furnishings and equipment for educational needs; includes a computer carrel for
wheelchair height.

GlasTec
P.O. Box 28
Middlebury, IN 46540
(800) 348-7464
Plumbing fixtures with adjustable features.

Guardian Products, Inc.
Sunrise Medical
12800 Wentworth Street
Box C-4522
Arleta, CA 91331-4522
(818) 504-2820
Bathing and transfer aids, ramps, walkers.

Hammatt Senior Products
P.O. Box 727
Mount Vernon, WA 98273
(206) 428-5850
Recreation products including games, records, tapes, videos.

Home Care Equipment
Wheelchair Carrier Inc.
P.O. Box 79
726 Farnsworth Road
Waterville, OH 43556-0079
Walkers, bath and shower seats, bathtub rails, wheelchair and walker accessories, exercise videos.

Independent Living Aids, Inc.
27 East Mall
Plainview, NY 11803
(800) 537-2118
Watches, clocks, and timers, lighting, Braille items, portable electronic magnifiers, large print books and calculators, game and hobby items, kitchen items and housewares, telephones, security devices, bath and shower rails, grab bars, and benches.

LS&S Group, Inc.
P.O. Box 673
1808-G Janke Drive
Northbrook, IL 60062
(800) 468-4789
Specializing in products for the visually impaired. Watches and clocks, remote control speaker phone, calculators, telephones, appliances, talking smoke alarm, much more.

Lumex
Division of Lumex, Inc.
100 Spence Street
Bay Shore, NY 11706
(800) 645-5272

Bathroom safety products: grab bars and safety rails; bath seats; transfer benches; toilet seats; shower chairs. Walking aids: walkers, canes, and accessories. Wheelchairs.

Option Central
1604 Carroll Avenue
Green Bay, WI 54304
Housewares, personal items, recreation products, Braille writing products.

Pressalit
Dansk Pressalit A/S
August Enforgade 11-13
DK 8000 Arthus C
Denmark
Adjustable height lavatories.

Raymo Products, Inc.
212 South Blake
Olathe, KS 66061
(913) 782-1515
Wheelchair and walker accessories, lap desks.

Rifton®
Route 213
Rifton, NY 12471
(914) 658-3141
Shower and bath chairs, positioning and therapy devices, furnishings.

Science Products
Box 888
Southeastern, PA 19399
(800) 888-7400
"Sensory aids" including large print books, large print/talking calculators, talking scales and thermometers, tactile and sensory books, recreation equipment, large print typewriter, computer and TV screen magnifiers.

SelfCare Catalog
349 Healdsburg Avenue
Healdsburg, CA 95448
(800) 345-3371
Books, videos, home furnishings.

TASH Inc.
Technical Aids & Systems for the Handicapped Inc.
70 Gibson Drive, Unit 12
Markham, Ontario L3R 4C2
Environmental controls, computer aids, communication and education aids.

Tubular Specialties Manufacturing, Inc.
13011 South Spring Street
Los Angeles, CA 90061
(800) 421-2961
Grab bars — colored and metal.

# Index